BUILD YOUR OWN TREEHOUSE

BUILD YOUR OWN TREEHOUSE

A Practical Guide

MAURICE BARKLEY

Sterling Publishing Co., Inc.
New York

ACKNOWLEDGMENTS

This book would not exist without the love and encouragement of my wife, Marie Kleinhenz-Barkley, our daughter and son in-law, Diane and Kevin Spacher, their sons, AJ and Sean, our son William Barkley, his daughter, Mary and his son David.

Special thanks to Emma J. Herries, Robin Pudetti and Ted Williams for help in a hundred ways.

Library of Congress Cataloging-in-Publication Data

Barkley, Maurice.
   Build your own treehouse : a practical guide / Maurice Barkley.
      p. cm.
   Includes index.
   ISBN-13: 978-1-4027-3777-0
   ISBN-10: 1-4027-3777-7
   1. Tree houses—Design and construction—Amateurs' manuals. I. Title.

TH4885.B37 2007
690.89—dc22

                                        2006029426

10 9 8 7 6 5 4 3 2 1

Published by Sterling Publishing Co., Inc.
387 Park Avenue South, New York, NY 10016
© 2007 by Maurice Barkley
Distributed in Canada by Sterling Publishing
c/o Canadian Manda Group, 165 Dufferin Street
Toronto, Ontario, Canada M6K 3H6
Distributed in the United Kingdom by GMC Distribution Services,
Castle Place, 166 High Street, Lewes, East Sussex, England BN7 1XU
Distributed in Australia by Capricorn Link (Australia) Pty. Ltd.
P.O. Box 704, Windsor, NSW 2756, Australia

Printed in China
All rights reserved

Sterling ISBN-13: 978-1-4027-3777-0
          ISBN-10: 1-4027-3777-7

For information about custom editions, special sales, premium and corporate purchases,
please contact Sterling Special Sales Department at 800-805-5489 or specialsales@sterlingpub.com

Book Design: Chrissy Kwasnik
Book Photography: Randy O'Rourke
Author Photo, p. 128: Karen A. Knight
Illustrator: Vic Kulihin

*This book is dedicated to the memory of Chelsea Rich,
November 10, 1994 – November 15, 2005.*

Her beautiful spirit still lingers in the trees.

*The world is so full
of a number of things,
I'm sure we should all
be as happy as kings.*

—Robert Louis Stevenson

CONTENTS

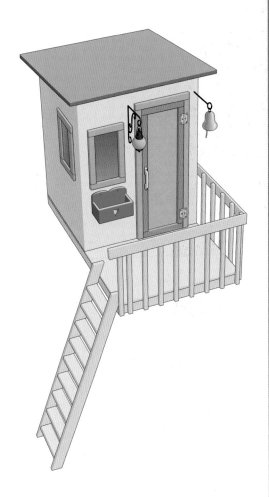

INSPIRATION

First, let me introduce myself. I am a seventy-three-year-old retired commercial artist, homeowner, family man, and since my sixty-fifth birthday, builder of treehouses.

My initial objective in writing this book was to create a permanent record of what I have built. In its earliest stages, this book was a scrapbook of pictures with my written comments intended primarily for my family and myself. But then the orientation shifted as I thought about the reactions of so many visitors of all ages to our treehouses. I wanted to spread the word about the wonderful experiences we have had thanks to our treehouses and encourage others to start building them too.

Most treehouse builders begin by standing in their back-yard staring at a tree or two, wondering whether the trees could support a treehouse and, if so, what the treehouse should look like. Probably there is a small child or a couple of children watching in not-so-quiet anticipation in the background.

Starting a structure with only an empty tree is a formidable task for most of us. Believe me, there was a time when I knew very little about tree structures myself. Here, I will do my best to tell you how it all began for me. If you are contemplating building your first treehouse, reading about my early struggles may give you some encouragement.

I did not start with a specific project or a request from a child—that came later. Several years ago, it occurred to me that the triple-trunk maple tree in my backyard would support a small platform. Why this thought came to me I suppose is because of my lifelong fascination with treehouses and the things that go with them—rope swings, bridges, secret clubs, and the sound of the wind on a quiet afternoon.

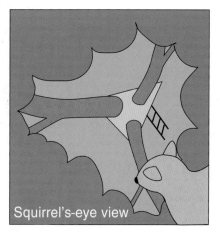

Squirrel's-eye view

First platform

The frame was rough-cut 2 x 4s nailed to the trunks. The floor was pieced together from used plywood. Not much, but it was a beginning.

A couple of years later, my grandsons began playing on my little platform 6 feet off the ground, and with a rope wrapped around the outside of all three trunks, they were able to stand safely in the middle. Eventually they began to talk of wanting something more.

Once I began, it went rather well. The new platform had posts that reached the ground. I used no nails this time (I believe the tree has forgiven me for the first platform).

My audience expands along with my building

Platform with bridge

The bridge was more difficult. After a good deal of trial and error, I settled on a design I have used successfully ever since. The bridge design is beyond the scope of this book, however. Here I cover platforms and the basic treehouse.

As good fortune would have it, the completion of the project coincided with my sixty-fifth birthday and my semiretirement, which gave me the gift of time.

You see, while building this platform and bridge, I came to realize that this was enormously fun and gratifying. The act of doing broke down some mental barriers, and ideas began to take shape automatically in my mind. I loved doing this. I could not stop, so I set my sights on the next tree and never looked back, except to admire what I had built.

I have learned many things through trial and error and the experience of doing. I'm sure, based on my own experience, that there are aspects to consider that are obscure to the beginner. I hope you can take advantage of my journey and avoid some of the pitfalls and ladder falls along the way. And I hope that building treehouses will be as gratifying for you as it has been for me.

CHAPTER 1

CHOOSING a TREE

I read once somewhere (I think the author was expounding on DNA) that a tree is nothing more than a rather complex blade of grass. From a tree's point of view, its job is to grow and make seeds of one form or another—that's it. All of the different woods, leaves, flowers, and seeds work to the same end. Natural selection has allowed trees to adapt to all but the most hostile environments.

WHAT TREES ARE BEST

Sometime ago, a visitor to my treehouses asked me what trees would be best should he decide to build his own tree-house. Knowing that he had a home in the suburbs, I told him that the ideal trees would be those that were now growing on his property. This is true for most of us who do not own farms or other large pieces of land.

Of course, you could go to your nearby garden center, buy four or five nice young oak trees, plant them in an attractive group in your yard, step back and admire them for sixty or seventy years, and then start building. Get the idea? If you have a perfect tree, lucky for you, but there is a good chance that all you have is a row of poplars and a smallish plain tree. The point is to work with what you've got.

TREES ARE HEAVY!

One thing of note that I learned long ago is how surprisingly heavy a tree can be. If you have ever cut timber for any reason, you know this to be true. That good-size tree you may have seen leaning over someone's house can weigh three, four, or five times as much as that honkin' big SUV driving by your home. If you build in a leaning tree, you may be activating the trigger. In other words, be careful.

There are several ways to incorporate the trees you have into your grand scheme with minimal impact to the trees involved.

- There are trees that can carry the entire load.
- Structures might be hung between two trees.
- You might use a self-supporting platform with a tree growing up through its middle.

A vertical post may take part or most of the load with the tree providing lateral support.

If your trees are too small, a self-supporting structure could snuggle up to them without leaning on them.

In one case, I have a young locust tree tied to a vertical post that supports a small platform. I expect it to grow up and around the little structure.

Now, as you evaluate the candidate tree or trees, there are things you must consider.

If you don't know the name of the tree you are looking at, find out. A quick jaunt on the Internet should help you identify it.

When you build a structure in a tree, you are adding weight and, more significantly, you are presenting to the wind what is in effect a sail. Wind is much more powerful than most of us realize and is often the trigger that will bring a tree down. Disease, injury, shallow roots, changing soil conditions, a significant lean, or even natural growth may create the conditions that allow the wind to destroy a particular tree. As a tree grows, it becomes more top-heavy and presents a greater surface for the wind to push on. Picture a little leaf fluttering in a strong breeze. The resistance or push may be only one ounce, but the tree could have ten thousand leaves—that's ten thousand ounces, which translates into, well, a lot. You may have heard that some trees are used as windbreaks. This comes at a price to the tree in question. If it survives, it is often deformed. Keep in mind that a tree, like any living thing, has a cycle of life and is affected constantly by external events. That big tree in your yard will not last forever.

Here is a very general list of suitable (good) trees and a list of unsuitable (bad) trees.

GOOD TREES	BAD TREES
• Apple	• Aspen
• Ash	• Birch
• Beech	• Black walnut
• Cedar	• Box elder
• Colorado blue spruce	• Cottonwood
• Cypress	• Maple (Silver)
• Fir	• Poplar and Lombardy poplar
• Hemlock	• Spruce (other than Colorado)
• Hickory	• Virginia pine
• Maple (Sugar)	
• Oak	

I could have included locust trees in the "bad" list because they have thorns. However, I have two of these trees close together in my side yard. They are host to an aerial deck and two houses. In the spring, I remove thorns from the new growth that is in reach of little fingers.

If your tree is not on either of these lists, you can search for it on the Internet.

Keep in mind that this book deals with small treehouses, so we are not necessarily looking for very large, mature trees. Picture the proposed structure 10 to 15 feet high as you investigate. Smaller well-branched trees are the ideal.

Look for deadwood, which could be a sign of disease. I have some Norway maples. They have smaller limbs that die

KNOW YOUR ROOTS

Tree roots do not grow down as far as the tree grows up. Very few trees have a taproot.

Roots require oxygen and water to survive.

As many as 90 percent of all roots are in the top 6 to 24 inches of soil.

Roots cannot detect water— they simply grow in moist soil and stop growing when dry.

Roots do not grow toward anything or in any particular direction.

Roots consist of large perennial roots and small short-lived feeder roots.

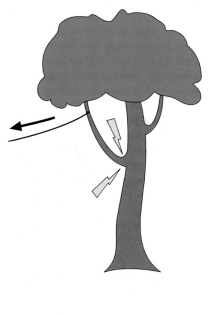

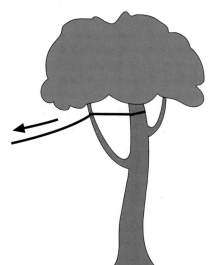

off constantly, but this seems to be a natural process. Look for splits in crotches. These could hide internal decay. If a branch will be used for critical as opposed to redundant support, you must plan to give it additional support by cable from overhead or a post from below.

Some things, I think, come down to common sense—for example, let us say that I have a hand rope for a bridge tied to a branch, as shown in the illustration at top left.

Note that in this instance the hand rope is pulling the branch away from the tree, creating extra strain on the crotch. This is unnecessary and potentially dangerous. The solution is shown in the next drawing.

Here, the rope is supported only vertically by the branch. Almost all of any pull is taken by the main trunk. I have done this in several places in my complex. If a branch has to assume the entire load of an object, I always provide backup support from either above or below.

Since I build on a small scale, I am not very concerned with how fast a tree grows. It is fairly easy to adjust suspension ropes and cables. After six years, only one house slung between two trees is beginning to tilt very slightly. Frankly, my main concern after safety is to minimize any damage to the tree.

Take your time in choosing a location. When you do find a likely spot, go get a lawn chair, a pad and a pencil, and a cup of tea. Your job is to construct an image in your mind of what you would like to build. How high off the ground should it be? Do you want to use a ladder or steps? What type of platform do you want? In this planning stage, the house needs only to be a dimensional box, unless, of course, you have a particular design in mind. Don't worry if your sketch is lacking in artistic merit. It is for your use in building, not to be framed and hung on the wall. At right is a sketch for one of my treehouses. You need to visualize only the essential components at this time.

Sketch of idea for treehouse

Your little drawings will help you build the project before-hand in your head, thus discovering problems well ahead of construction. When you are satisfied, flip to the appropriate section and prepare to build.

Specific methods of supporting various structures in a variety of different trees are covered in detail in this book.

CHAPTER 2

SAFETY

Every list you make while planning or building should have SAFETY in large letters at the top. Safety boils down to knowledge and common sense tempered by experience. There are two main safety considerations: safety while building and the safety of those who use what you build. In taking precautions, I have made a special effort to follow certain routines I have developed through experience.

SAFETY WHILE BUILDING

I have been constructing treehouses now for seven years, and so far, so good. However, one mistake, one careless or hurried movement, could end my treehouse-building days. There are three big Bear Traps hidden out there in the tall grass just waiting for you, the builder. They are labeled Unexpected, Distracted, and Careless.

The unexpected could be a strong-looking limb that suddenly gives way. I have such a limb that is home to a long and very popular rope swing. It has held up well, but it has a strong cable up there giving extra support to the limb. I have several bridges going from tree to tree. The ropes providing the support are stronger than necessary, so to see one of them break would be unexpected, to say the least, but just in case, each bridge is supported by eight ropes.

Watch Out!

Here are two examples of the unexpected and a distraction. Perhaps you can learn from them so that you can avoid such incidents yourself.

One day I was up on a ladder replacing a stabilizing hemp rope. I was following all of my common-sense safety rules, but what I didn't know was that there was a robin's nest out of sight but quite close to where I was at work. Now, a robin or most any bird will do its level best to avoid all human contact, unless you come close to an occupied nest. The robin flew in from the rear and with one wing gave me a solid swat on the top of my head. At that moment, I was reaching up to untie the old rope. My hands jerked back to ward off the attack, and I lost my balance. Thank heavens for my homemade safety belt.

The only other similar incident was with hornets that I encountered while painting under the eaves of one of my treehouses, again on my ladder. A paint spill was the worst of that incident, thanks again to my safety belt and a hasty retreat down the ladder. You must keep a constant watch for wasps and hornets. Get rid of them right away—show no mercy.

As for carelessness, don't you just hate it when you do something dumb because you were lazy or in a hurry? There was a day and an occurrence that will live in infamy, and worse, my wife knows all about it because she came to my rescue.

I was installing a new bridge. The walking-surface planks and the hand ropes were in place. All that remained was the installation of the vertical ropes that tie the hand rope to the base. I have a system that works well for those who follow it. I start in the center of the bridge, where I install five of these ropes. I then climb down, move the ladder to one side, climb up, and install three ropes. I climb down, move to other side, climb up, and install three more. Using this back-and-forth method, I continue until the job is finished. It would be much faster if I could do four or five ropes instead of three, right? Yes, right you are, except for the problem of balance.

I had decided to lean to one side to install an extra rope, and the ladder started to tilt in the direction I was leaning. Leaning too far, I grabbed on to the walking surface of the bridge, but one leg got hooked in the ladder, preventing me from dropping the 4 feet to the ground without breaking a leg. There I hung with the ladder at a 45-degree angle. Shaking my leg only made it worse. Some loud calls for help brought my wife, who quickly removed the ladder like a growth from my leg and steadied me as I descended to earth. Only then did her laughter begin.

LADDERS

Stepladders

Stepladders are indispensable, but they also are treacherous, so it helps to follow a routine regardless of the pressures of time. Even with an aluminum stepladder, things can happen. The front legs can kick out if the ladder is not set square on the ground, for example. Here's a good routine to follow.

1. Place the ladder exactly where you need it.
2. If the ground is irregular, level the rear legs with old boards of different thicknesses; then do the same thing if there is a hanging front leg. If the ground is soft, use boards under all the legs.
3. Once the ladder looks secure, climb up one step, grab the top in the middle, and lean back to lift the front legs momentarily by pulling the top toward you. This will straighten the legs if they are cocked.

Extension Ladders

Even the best extension ladder is a dangerous device, especially when it's leaning against some part of a tree instead of the nice flat wall of a house. The stability of an extension ladder depends on the bottom legs resting level on solid ground. Make sure the ground does not yield. The top legs

push out equally, and if, for example, a branch gives way, on one leg the ladder can spin as much as 180 degrees, because you, the climber on top of the ladder, create an imbalance every time you go up. If this should happen, there you are, dangling from what is now the underside of the ladder or worse, crumpled on the ground. Again, follow a routine.

1. Place the ladder carefully exactly where you need it.
2. Make sure the ground does not yield.
3. Climb a couple of rungs, and wiggle the ladder around a bit to test its stability.

Ladder Safety

Think "slow motion" going up or down. Keep three limbs in contact with the rungs at all times, right down to the last step. Ladder safety is seriously important. Below is a list that summarizes what you need to know.

- Buy only high-quality extension ladders and stepladders.
- Scaffolding is wonderful if you can afford it.
- Extension ladders are long enough to touch overhead electric wires.
- Place legs on planks when soil is wet or soft.
- Use guides printed on ladder sides for placement angles and weight limits.
- Place the ladder top securely. If necessary, tie it off.
- Remember that the forward thrust of a ladder increases as you climb.
- Don't climb with muddy shoes.
- Always climb with free hands. Use a tool belt or haul tools up with a rope.
- Three limbs should be in contact with rungs at all times.
- Use a safety hook while working.
- Do not work fast or move fast.
- Climb down as you climbed up. Never face outward.
- Climb all the way down. Never, ever jump the last few rungs.

- Always look down. Ground contact can be jarring if you thought the last step you took was just another rung and you didn't expect to hit the ground.
- Use large rubber bands on cuffs of pants to avoid snags. Ditto for your flannel shirt.
- Know exactly what the job is before you climb.
- Any parts that can be done on the ground should definitely be worked on there.
- Make sure you have all necessary tools.
- Don't lean. If necessary, climb down and move the ladder.
- When moving extension ladders, be sure to compress them for balance.
- When picking up a long ladder from the ground, move to the top end, pick it up, walk it to vertical, and then place it where needed.
- Never leave the ladder up when unattended.
- Never allow two people on the ladder at the same time.
- The little kids in your treehouse have no reason to be on a work ladder. Make sure you tell them.
- Ladders are expensive. Paint your name on the side, and be cautious about lending it. Well-intentioned people can damage your tools.
- Aluminum ladders have hollow rungs. Check them once in a while for wasp nests.
- Do not a use a ladder as a scaffold plank. Use all tools for the jobs for which they are intended.
- Remember that gravity is with you every second. It will bring you or tools to the ground if you get careless.
- Keep your first aid kit handy.
- Keep emergency phone numbers in your wallet.
- Wear prescription or safety glasses.
- Use a dust mask when sawing treated lumber.
- Use a block and tackle for heavy lifting.
- Quit when you get tired.
- Never leave power tools unattended around your ladder or anywhere else.
- Never work alone while on a ladder.

TOOL BELTS

Tool belts are indispensable for safety. Your hands need to be free, especially when you are climbing a ladder. Nevertheless, you don't need to buy an expensive tool belt. You can make your own.

Drill a hole through the handle of your hammer at the end opposite the head, and loop a short cord through the new hole and tie a tight knot. Now punch some holes through an old leather belt. Take a wire coat hanger, and with pliers make the hook shown at left. Make as many as you like. It's okay to be decked out like a Christmas tree.

Do what you have to do to keep your hands free.

Attach a short rope to the front of the leather belt. This rope ought to have a stronger hook on its end. That way, when you reach your working height, you can put the hook over one rung. This will keep you from leaning back too far when working with both hands.

Hooks and belt

BRANCH SAFETY

Never trust small or dead branches. Even a nice strong-looking branch may have hidden flaws, and usually when a branch decides to give up, it doesn't sag or give a warning, but just snaps and collapses along with anything it supports. If you use a side branch for critical support, always provide backup support with a cable or a post.

BUILDING SAFETY INTO EACH STRUCTURE

Make sure that there is nowhere that a child can leave any structure without deliberately climbing over a barrier. The only way to go up or down should be on a ladder or stairs. Careful planning can reduce dramatically the risks encountered by children. Below is a general list of ways to maintain a safe treehouse environment. More structural safety issues are covered in the section on maintenance at the end of the chapter.

- Children are not as smart as you, except maybe with computers. You must remain in charge.
- Limit the number of occupants at any one time.
- Use removable ladders, and remember to remove them when you are not at home.
- Enlist friendly neighbors to keep an eye on things.
- Always require permission, even from the kids next door.
- Let everyone know that if you are not at home, the treehouse is off-limits.
- Inspect the treehouse after each visit so that you know whom to blame for this or that.
- No fire ever (birthday cakes, etc.).
- No running. No acrobatics.
- No access when it is raining.

GRAVITY WARS
(How to Lift Heavy Things without Hurting Yourself)

Levers

If you own a wheelbarrow, take a look at it. It's a fine example of two levers and a wheel. Although very useful, it is inherently an unstable device because the load is usually above the wheel and the line of the handles. You are in effect balancing the load while you are pushing it around.

Often it's necessary to use a lever to move something. If you have used a toothpick, you have used a lever. In any case, this is a good place to include a quick lesson on the common lever.

Gather up two pencils and a wad of clay the size of a tennis ball. Lay the first pencil (fulcrum) almost touching the clay as shown in A at the bottom of the next page.

Pick up the second pencil (lever), and jam the point well into the clay, as shown (B).

Press down on the eraser of the second pencil. The clay will rise with ease until the eraser touches the surface (C).

Now raise the end of the lever pencil, and move the first (fulcrum) pencil away from the clay to within an inch of the eraser; then press down as before (D).

Suddenly the clay gains a lot of weight. This demonstrates that as you move a fulcrum closer to the object being moved, the object becomes easier to lift.

Here's a real-world example. Say, in building your tree-house, you have to lift a 4 × 4 vertical post that connects a rope bridge to a maple tree. Since the bridge moves slightly in the wind, the post has shifted a bit and you have to move it approximately 3 inches back to the center of the cement pylon on which it rests. The weight bearing down on the pylon is approximately 200 pounds. Never try to lift it yourself. Instead, use a lever.

Drill a ⅜-inch hole approximately 6 inches from the bottom of the post, and temporarily insert a ½-inch lag screw approximately halfway. Then place a cinder block next to the pylon perpendicular to the desired line of movement, and add scrap lumber to just below the level of the lag screw. Remember that you have to lift the post only a fraction of an inch in order to shift it.

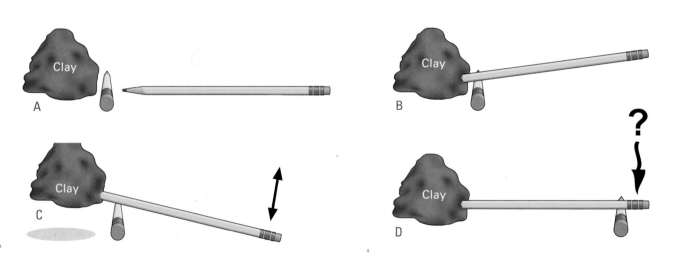

When you tuck the long 2 × 4 under the lag screw, all you have to do is step on it approximately 3 feet out and the post is lifted. Shift your foot and move the post to where you want it, and then raise your leg, and you're done. You'll work harder getting up off the couch.

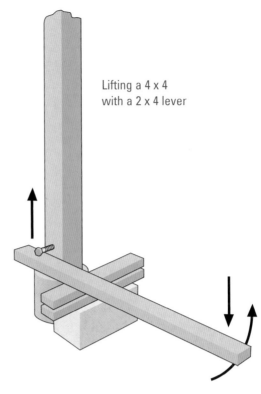

Lifting a 4 x 4
with a 2 x 4 lever

Block and Tackle

There are times when a heavy object must be lifted more than a few inches, maybe 10 feet up in a tree. The object could be long as well as heavy, perhaps to go between two trees.

Say hello to a block and tackle. This is not a football maneuver, but a mechanical device of ropes, pulleys, and hooks. You will find a wide variety of these at your local hardware store. Mine has four pulley wheels (two on each end) and a locking device. It has a 1-ton load limit, which is quite a bit more than the loads I deal with.

Here we go with another real-world example, this one on the use of the block and tackle. Your task is to lift a heavy wood beam (approximately 250 pounds) to its new home approximately 12 feet up between two trees.

Begin by moving the beam from my driveway to between the two trees. You can do this easily by using two hand trucks as shown at the top of the next page.

Using two 4-foot lengths of ½-inch rope, tie each one (square knot, please) to make two loops (one for each end of the beam). Place each rope approximately 12 inches from each end, as shown below at left. Also, add two fence staples to hold the rope in place.

When that's done, rope your block and tackle to a convenient limb, and then hoist one end up to the required height. Once there, tie the beam end to the tree, and then lift the other end.

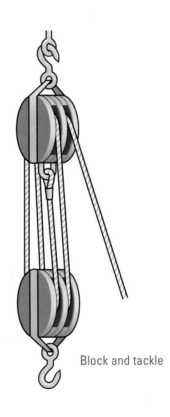

Block and tackle

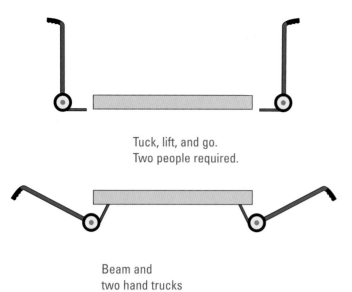

Tuck, lift, and go.
Two people required.

Beam and
two hand trucks

In conclusion, I would like to say that there are many ways to accomplish these tasks. Each lifting challenge you face will most likely be unique in terms of detail, but the fundamentals remain the same. Think before you move. Plan the entire move before you start. Take your time. If you are in a hurry or agitated, you invite disaster. When in doubt, stop and get help or rethink the job. There is a great deal of satisfaction in working out this type of problem. Do it well, do it intelligently, and do it safely.

A WORD ON MAINTENANCE

Every darn winter morning, I climb on my darn stationary bicycle and pump away for 30 minutes; not 29 minutes, 30 minutes.

I tell myself that this is simply what I do. It is a part of my morning ritual. I get up, have some coffee and toast, ride the bike, and then have a second cup of coffee.

There are things you do that should become a ritual—such as maintenance. Maintenance is making sure things are in

Rope on beam

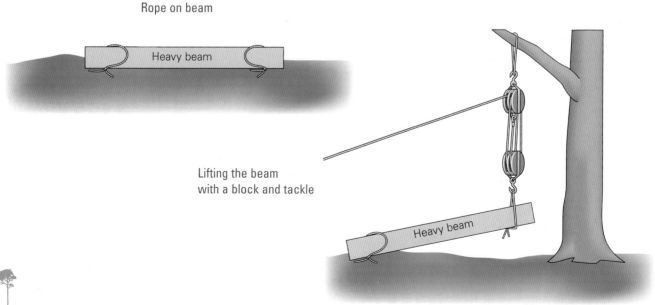

Lifting the beam
with a block and tackle

good working order. The benefit of good maintenance is safety, so make it a ritual—it's just what you do.

At least once a month, look at the ropes, the bridge planks, the bridge anchors, the stabilizing cables, and the mounts of the various platforms. If you examine these things fairly often, you will notice when something changes. I carry a long pole so that anything that looks suspicious gets a good poke. The old saying "A stitch in time saves nine" really applies to maintaining a treehouse. A little bit at a time makes the maintenance easy and keeps the little things little.

Once a year, each spring, you should get out your ladder and take a close, critical look at everything structural. Make a hands-on check of all bolts and cables. Examine all platforms, with particular attention to bridge anchors. One thing of particular interest is any place where a rope goes through a hole. Take a close look because here is where a rope can fray first and where it can fail first. I have never had a rope failure, because there are no ropes older than five years in my treehouse village.

If you use nails, they can raise and become a snag or tripping hazard. I don't know the cause, but a few minutes with a hammer will fix the problem.

When you are examining any part of your treehouse, keep picturing a very young child hurrying about, having fun, and not paying attention. A growing branch making its way through the slats of a bridge may be attractive, but it is also a tripping hazard.

Once you've done all of that, get out the paint can and make the weathered parts sparkle.

CHAPTER 3

TOOLS and MATERIALS

The Blue Ribbon goes to the battery-operated drill, my favorite tool. Once you buy one, it becomes indispensable. Not only do these beauties save wear and tear on your wrists; they also eliminate the need to drag long extension cords all over the place. If you can, buy two: one with a drill bit for pilot holes and the other with a bit to drive deck screws.

TOOLS

As with so many other things in life, there is no one-size-fits-all box of tools that will do the job for everyone. Some builders may have a complete workshop, while others may have little or nothing. Most will be somewhere in the middle.

Without these tools, you could build a treehouse, but it would be much more difficult and time consuming. For example, rather than using a big 4-foot wallboard T square, you can always use the edges of an uncut sheet of plywood, because these things are reliably cut at 90 degrees. A Phillips screwdriver is in the list on page 24 because deck screws are better than nails, but you can see that a battery-operated drill is far superior in every respect.

DECK SCREWS

Deck screws work better than nails. They hold well and make repairs and replacements easier. Use deck screws, not nails. Try square-drive screws instead of Phillips.

BASIC REQUIREMENTS

Here is a very bare-bones list—an absolute minimum for building anything you see in this book.

Ladders—extension and step to fit height

Handsaw

Phillips screwdriver

Electric drill and bits (preferably the battery-operated model)

Claw hammer

Vise grips

Pocketknife

Tape measure—20 to 30 feet

Level

Carpenter's square—24 inches

ADDITIONAL TOOLS

A slightly more fleshed-out list might include the following:

- Ladders—extension and step to fit height
- Battery-operated drills
- Saws—two handsaws, hacksaw, pole saw, gig saw, reciprocating saw, hole saw, skill saw, small table saw, chop saw, and chain saw
- Bench grinder
- Hammers—claw, small sledge, and hatchet
- Screwdrivers—set
- Files and rasps
- Pliers—regular, needle-nose, and cutting
- Wrenches—crescent, monkey, vise-grip, set of open-end and socket
- Anvil pruning shears, to cut rope and twigs
- Pocketknife
- Tape measures—48 inches and 20 to 30 feet
- Wallboard T squares—regular (24 inches) and 4 feet
- Levels—straight, line, and plum bob (made with kite string and a heavy nut)
- Pry bar
- Block and tackle
- Pencil and notebook (helpful for jotting down measurements while high in a tree)
- Tool belt

Once you get going, you will want a carpenter's apron and a leather belt with hooks. The apron pockets hold the small stuff such as screws, and the belt hooks hold the big stuff; the belt should also have a hook to fasten on a ladder rung while you work. Your pockets will soon fill up with lots of tools, but be sure to leave room for some peanuts. Remember that you are a visitor in the trees and the squirrels that live there expect some tribute.

A battery-powered drill (screwdriver) is a wonderful tool.

PILOT HOLES 🏠

Pilot holes are the holes you make to prepare the way for the deck screw. Be sure that you get the gauge right— neither too big nor too small for the screw.

MATERIALS

What follow are again two lists: one for the basic structure and the other for houses and ornaments that sit on the basic structure. Basic structure means all bridges, permanent staircases, and platforms for houses and aerial decks—all things that provide critical support and are assumed to be exposed permanently to the weather. You must not skimp on basic support.

MATERIALS FOR BASIC STRUCTURE

Deck screws—Phillips square drive, formulated for pressure-treated lumber.

One small box each of 1 inch, 1¼ inches, and 2½ inches, and three boxes of 3 inches. (Buy more as you need them.)

PLATFORM MATERIAL

(All 3 versions are discussed in Chapter 5; Version 2 is the focus of Chapter 6, and Version 3 of Chapter 7.)

(Lumber should be good-quality exterior, rated for ground contact.)

½-inch exterior plywood.

One 4 x 8 foot sheet.

2 x 6 x 8 pressure-treated lumber.

Five each. (Two of these could be longer depending on the distance between trees.)

2 x 4 x 8 pressure-treated lumber.

1 for Version 2, 2 for Version 3.

4 x 4 x ? pressure-treated landscape timber.

These are the legs, if needed. Length depends on platform height.

Galvanized lag screws with washer.

Version 1—16 each of ½ x 4 inches.

Version 2—16 each of ½ x 4 inches, four each of ½ x 6 inches.

Version 3—16 each of ½ x 4 inches, eight each of ½ x 6 inches.

½-inch-diameter eyebolt with 3 inches of thread. Nut and washer.

Four each. (These are used only with Version 1.)

³/₁₆-inch stainless-steel cable.

740 lb. test.

20 feet for Version 2.

40 feet for Version 1.

³/₁₆-inch cable clamps and thimbles.

10 each for Version 2.

20 each for Version 3.

HOUSE MATERIAL

¹⁄₄ inches x 4 x 8 regular luan plywood.

Six each.

2 x 3 x 8 common pine.

Nine each.

1 x 3 x 8 common pine strapping lumber.

Six each for door, two each for each window.

Box hinges.

Two each (approximately 4 inches or less—size not critical).

Screen door spring and stand-off.

One each.

Aluminum screening.

14 x 22-inch piece for each window.

Fibered roof coating (and paint thinner and a stiff-bristled brush).

One gallon.

(Of course, you may use shingles, but, if so, you must use ¹⁄₂-inch plywood for the top and very short nails so that they will not penetrate to the interior. Shingles are heavy.)

STEPS MATERIAL

1 x 6 x ? standard deck lumber.

Two lengths 12 inches longer than the height of your platform. Six step boards can be cut from one 1 x 6 x 8.

1 x 4 x 8 plain exterior lumber (for risers).

Same number as steps.

Handy 4-inch hanging hook.

Two each

PORCH-RAILING MATERIAL

2 x 2 x 8 exterior pole lumber.

Cut three 32-inch lengths from five pieces.

1 x 4 x 8 plain exterior lumber.

Two each (for railings).

Waterproof glue (optional).

Exterior paint of your choice.

The material used in the houses is a different matter. A house supports only its own walls and roof. This means you may use less-expensive new or recycled things. You will see mention of this more than once in this book. Look for usable junk, clean it, cut it, apply it, and see it as part of a new treehouse.

MATERIALS FOR THE HOUSE

Not much here in the way of rocket science—just practical things to use on a regular basis.

    All plywood.
    All lumber.
    Old roofing and fibered roof tar.
    Screening.
    Tubing.
    Belts, wheels, and gears.
    Old doors and hardware.
    Assorted nails and screws.
    Anything that looks interesting but is not too big or heavy.
    Plexiglas or screening. (No old windows—glass is not suitable.)

COSTS

Something old, something new, something borrowed, and a bottle of glue.

When it comes to the cost of materials, two distinct categories should be considered. First is the cost of structural items. Second is the cost of houses and other things that rest on the basic structure.

Ropes, cables, bridge planks, hardware, beams, walkways, railings, and house floors must be high quality. Use pressure-treated and relatively knot-free exterior lumber. The cable I use is galvanized, 1/4-inch, 740-pound test. Stainless steel is available in some sizes, but it is more expensive and a bit less strong. For appearance's sake, use brown or black rope. Nylon rope is best for longevity but comes in white or bright colors.

When using a mix of vinyl and hemp rope, you must replace the ropes every three to five years.

You cannot cut corners on anything that provides basic support. Building something stronger than necessary is good.

I could easily go over to my neighborhood supply center and provide a dollar amount for all of the materials listed here, but the only guarantee is that by the time anyone reads this the price will have changed—possibly by a significant amount. Why, I remember once having bought a loaf of bread for 15 cents. It was the same day I paid 23 cents for a gallon of gas for my father's 1939 Plymouth.

It would still be a good idea to take a casual stroll through your supply store with a list of materials and a notepad to estimate the treehouse cost. Besides, it's fun. And you may well see something that you never knew you needed until you saw it there on the shelf.

Regarding the cost of houses and other things that rest on the basic structure, I can save you a significant amount of money.

ONE PERSON'S JUNK IS ANOTHER PERSON'S TREASURE

The things people throw away are truly amazing. At right you see a giant old clock at the entrance to a bridge. It was an advertising display at a local bank. When they finished with it, I asked for it and they were glad to get rid of it. This clock hung on our living-room wall for several years and then went into storage in the basement until I built a bridge and had an inspiration.

I made the Yellow Brick Road, also shown in Chapter 10, from bricks picked up from the side of the road. Odd pieces of plywood and lumber came from the same source. During my working years, some of my business clients gave me access to their Dumpsters/treasure chests. From them came

more plywood and lumber, pulleys for small hand-operated lift baskets, window screening, half cans of paint, electrical wire, hinges, bolts, nuts, screws, and even mysterious small machines that must do something but no one knows what.

As an example, let me tell you about the material I used to build Miss Mary's Teahouse. The roof beams are salvaged 2×3s covered by thin plywood cut from some old closet doors. The six skylights are large coffee cans with their original clear plastic covers. All of this is painted black with inexpensive fibered roof coating.

The eight wall panels are framed with 1×4 common pine lumber (this I had to buy). The lower half of each is salvage plywood with a square plastic ornament in the center that I cut from the arms of an old sofa and easy chair. Above that are grills that had a former life above our kitchen cabinets. I put salvaged wooden shingles above the grillwork and then painted everything with bargain paint. (When the paint store makes a mistake while mixing a color, they sell the result really cheap. Just don't be fussy about exact colors.) Inside I built small seats from more scrap plywood and covered them with pieces of leftover carpet. The entrance is a Dutch door. In the top center, I put a large lens from an old copy machine. Below that, I mounted an old doorknocker once used on the front door of our house. The door handle is a piece of a branch from a peach tree.

CHAPTER 4

START BUILDING

There comes a point when it is time to pick up your tools and build something simple and relatively easy. As this may be your first attempt, it is important that you succeed in creating a sturdy and safe treehouse for yourself and the welfare of those who may use it. This could be the only treehouse you ever build, or it may be the first of many magic castles in the air.

PLANNING SO YOU CAN START BUILDING

There are options and variations presented here that will assist you in finalizing the design you use. Read this whole section through before making any decisions about the exact configuration of the project you want to start.

The entire project will be presented in four parts: (1) the platform on which the house sits, (2) the access to the house (stairs and ladders), (3) the house, and (4) accessories and decorations.

Item 1, the platform, is of the greatest concern and is the most complicated because of the wide variety of physical locations where people might build a treehouse. The plans presented here are suitable for most situations. Three basic plans will give you a choice to fit the situation you have. The

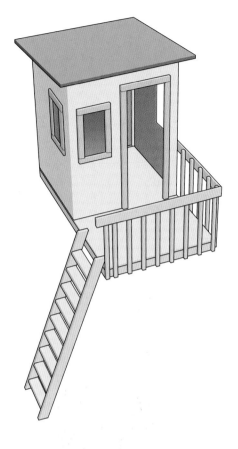

plans provide for a 4 × 4 foot house and a 4-foot x 30 inch porch.

Item 2, the access, involves detailed plans for steps to your treehouse.

Item 3, the house, will be a 4 × 4-foot box with a very simple roof. It will have a door and the option of one or more windows.

Item 4, the accessories and decorations, will be, for example a bucket on a rope, pegs for hanging things, small furniture, and so on.

TIME TO START BUILDING

Now that the time has come to actually build something, you may have doubts. Many who have gone before you have paddled the same boat. They did not know where to begin, where to middle, or where to end. Fortunately for you, your complete course has been charted in this book.

Here (above left) is a drawing of a basic treehouse in its simplest, undecorated form. This is to give you a look at your goal. Do not show it to your child just yet. If you do, your young one will want it in place before dark on the same day.

First and foremost, you must consider the platform. Think of a solid, twist-free wooden slab suspended in space.

It can move up and down (A).

It can swing side to side (B).

It can tilt in many ways (C).

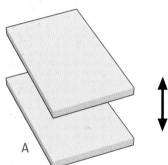

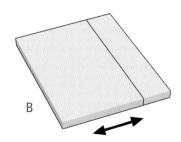

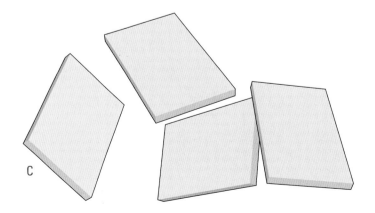

WHICH PLATFORM?

Keep all of this in mind as you proceed. The pages that follow detail, step-by-step, three methods of holding a platform safely and securely off the ground. There are literally hundreds of variations depending on terrain, tree size, shape, and location. But the three samples here should provide you with enough information so that if you have to modify or reconfigure a bit, you can do so safely and successfully with minimal impact to the tree.

Remember that gravity is a constant. You will be dealing with it every minute, not only regarding the treehouse and its parts, but also in terms of your own movements. Balance is another major factor.

For example, a support cable that is not quite vertical could be exerting a sideways pull in the direction of its lean as well as supporting its load. Think of these things while you plan and work. There is real danger if you get careless.

The three platform variations are picutred here.

Note: Not included here is a platform with the tree coming up through the middle, because in a small house the trunk takes up too much room.

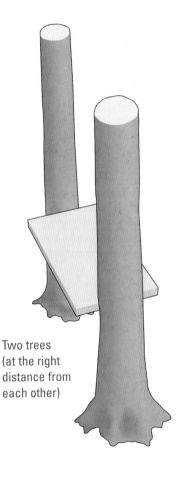

Two trees (at the right distance from each other)

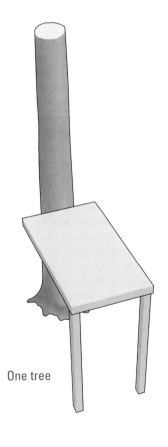

One tree

No tree

CHAPTER 5

BUILDING the PLATFORM

At this point, you have chosen one of the three versions and it is time to build a small, sturdy platform. If you have a chop saw that will cut square, it will make everything look and fit better. Make sure that you do not skimp on material. This is the basic support for whatever structure you are planning to build.

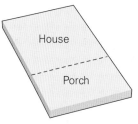

Platform with house and porch areas indicated

ASSEMBLE YOUR MATERIALS

Whichever version of platform you plan to build, you will need to have the materials at hand. See "Platform Material" on page 26 in Chapter 3 for the required materials.

Cut 1½ feet off of a 4 × 8 foot sheet of ½-inch or thicker plywood, for a platform of 4 × 6½ feet. This size is the same for all three versions. This yields 4 × 4 feet for the house and 4 × 2½ feet for the porch. You could get by with a 4 × 2 porch, but be assured that now and then an adult will just have to go up ther,e and these measurements provide room for a deck chair.

The platform floor is shown at top right.

The frame is shown in the next three illustrations. Use 2 × 6 pressure-treated knot-free exterior lumber. How it will look depends on the configuration you select.

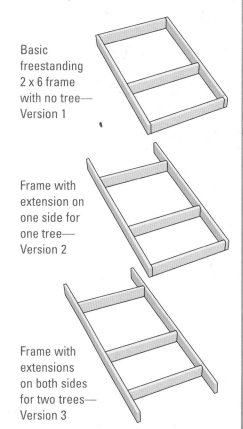

Basic freestanding 2 x 6 frame with no tree—Version 1

Frame with extension on one side for one tree—Version 2

Frame with extensions on both sides for two trees—Version 3

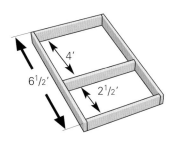

Version 1 measurements

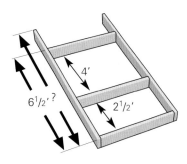

Version 2 measurements

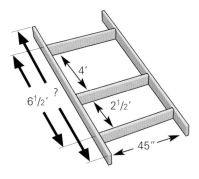

Version 3 measurements

The measurements labeled "?" in the frame illustrations above will be whatever you need for your particular application.

PLATFORM VARIATIONS

From four pieces of 2 × 6 lumber, cut the five pieces you need. All three versions have three lengths at 45 inches.

Version 1 has two lengths at 6½ feet.

Version 2 has two lengths at 6½ feet plus the diameter of the host tree plus 8 inches.

Version 3 has two lengths at the distance between the two trees plus their diameters plus 8 inches.

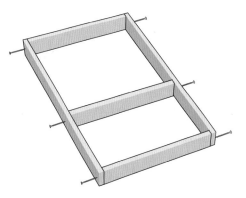

Screw locations on 2 x 6 frame

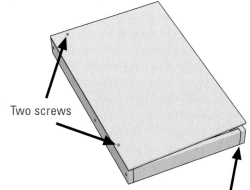

Two screws

Two screw locations

Tap square here, and then sink s crews all around.

Find a flat work surface, such as your driveway, and assemble the frame with six 4-inch deck screws. For Version 2, measure the 6½ foot platform length and screw the short length there. For Version 3, take into account the individual measurements of the trunk diameters to position the outer two shorter lengths (see page 53). Use only one screw in the center at each of these four locations so that the framework remains flexible until the top is applied.

Attach the plywood top to one of the longer sides with two 2-inch deck screws.

Tap the other side of the 2 × 6 box, square it with the plywood if necessary, and sink screws all around every 6 inches. Make sure that the plywood does not overlap the sides of the 2 × 6 box. If anything, it should be a bit short. Trim the plywood if necessary.

Drill two ⅜ × 4-inch pilot holes in each of four places, as shown below, and insert a ½ × 4-inch galvanized lag screw with washer in each. Draw them up tight until the washer begins to dent the wood.

There you have it—a solid, twist-free platform ready for its hardware and/or legs.

For Version 1, use 4 × 4-inch landscape timbers. Select timbers that are straight and relatively knot - free and have minimum checking (splitting the long way). The length of the timber will be determined by the height you choose.

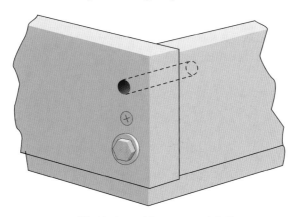

Pilot hole and lag screw detail

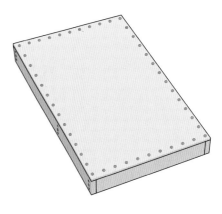

Finished platform

VERTICAL SUPPORT POSTS

Here are some important general considerations when choosing vertical support posts.

Say you have a 1 foot length of 4 × 4-inch post. If you stand it on end on a flat solid surface and have a pay loader lower its bucket filled with 2,000 pounds of gravel squarely on top of this poor 4 × 4, what happens? Nothing. The support is dealing only with the force of compression, and it does this quite well. We begin to have a problem when the post gets longer. The drawing at left shows a 12-foot post that has a slight warp. As weight is applied from above, the bend increases. If sufficient weight is applied (say, 2,000 pounds), the post will break, but not from compression.

This is the flaw in long thin lumber, which is why you are using 4 × 4 posts instead of 2 × 4s. The 2 × 4s can easily handle the compression forces applied here but would require long braces that will destroy the effect you are seeking.

Cut four 7 inch-pieces of 2 × 6 (spacer blocks). Cut four 5-inch pieces of 2 × 6 (spacer blocks). Note: The one-tree version will use only half the number of these pieces, and the two-tree version will use none as it has no legs.

Use one set of spacers (one 5-inch and one 7-inch) in each corner. This will greatly simplify the bracing for each leg. Use two each 2½-inches deck screws to hold each piece. (Screw them from the inside to hide the screw heads; the position is not critical.) The drawing at left shows how each corner should look.

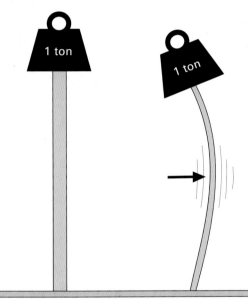

The 4 x 4 post supports weight; the thinner post could support compression, but bends due to warping flaws.

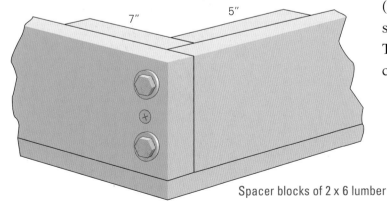

Spacer blocks of 2 x 6 lumber

If necessary, trim the four posts (legs) to the length you have chosen. Clamp each leg in place vertically, drill ⅜ × 4-inch pilot holes, and screw two galvanized lag screws with washers through the frame and spacer and into each leg. Check for vertical as you tighten each leg. Close is good enough. Note that the drawing at right shows the positions of the new lag screws. This is to avoid collision with the two lag screws in the frame. Remove the small deck screw.

MINIMIZING SWAY

The platform is now strong enough to hold Mr. Terwilliger, who weighs in excess of 250 pounds. What you must now provide for is balance.

When you are up on this type of platform, the last thing you want is to start swaying in any direction. You will agree that it spoils the experience. The fix is an angle brace that does not have to be very big.

When in place, the angle brace prevents movement from side to side. When you add a second angle brace, all lateral movement in any direction is stopped.

If you do this to all four legs, even Mr. Terwilliger couldn't make platform sway.

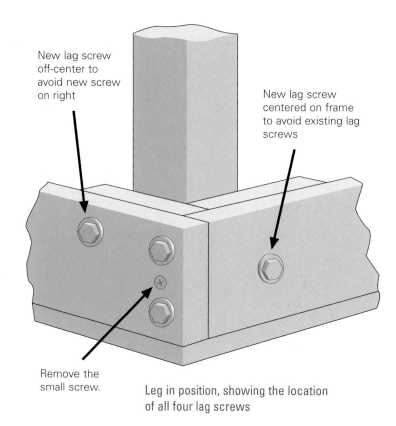

New lag screw off-center to avoid new screw on right

New lag screw centered on frame to avoid existing lag screws

Remove the small screw.

Leg in position, showing the location of all four lag screws

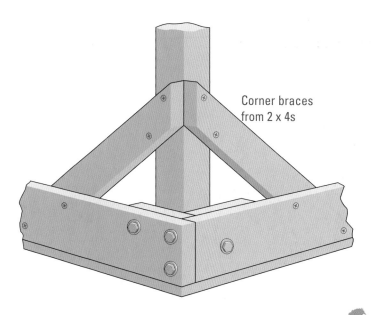

Corner braces from 2 x 4s

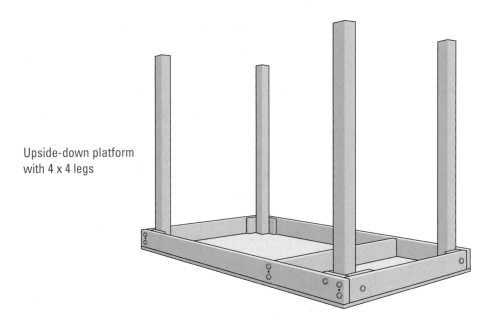

Upside-down platform
with 4 x 4 legs

Your platform is now lying upside down in your driveway—its legs sticking up in the air like an injured giraffe.

Cut three 32-inch lengths from each of three exterior 8-inch 2 × 4s. This yields nine pieces—you need eight. Save the ninth piece for use elsewhere. Cut each end of all eight boards 45 degrees, as shown here.

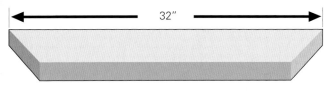

32"

Single 2 x 4 brace

Lay the brace in place, as shown at right. Slide the brace around until both angled faces rest firmly against the leg and the underside of the plywood top. Place a clamp, as shown, to hold the pieces while you work.

Sink two 3-inch deck screws through the brace and into the leg. Do this first, as the other end of the brace may shift a bit when the screws are tightened.

Then sink two 3-inch deck screws through the platform frame into the brace. Note that if the last two screws are a bit too long, the points will protrude from the wood on the inside, away from little fingers. Remove the clamp and repeat this process seven times.

The platform is finished.

Move it to your chosen location.

If you have firm, level soil, you can simply put the platform in place. If the soil is or can be soft, a square brick or a flat rock is usually sufficient to support it. Remember that this is not a permanent structure—it's okay if it sinks a bit. It is light enough to be adjusted at any time.

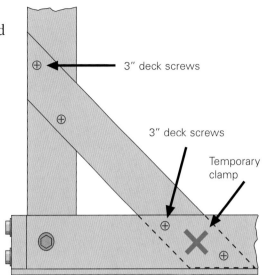

3″ deck screws

3″ deck screws

Temporary clamp

Angle brace with clamp

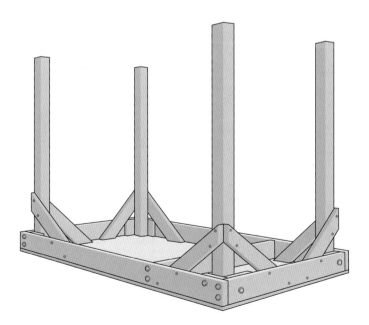

Finished platform, still upside down, showing all braces

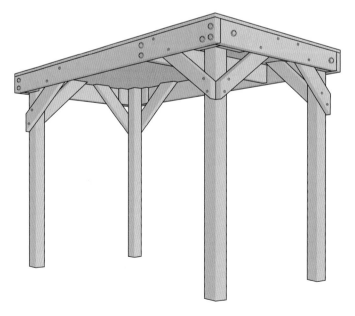

Platform turned upright

CHAPTER 6

THE PLATFORM in ONE TREE

A platform in one tree is our Version 2. You will need a platform with two legs on one end only. The tree end is supported primarily by a cable suspension system. The platform also has redundant support with a direct anchoring to the tree through the back frame. The anchoring secures the platform to the tree and eliminates sway.

Version 2 platform for one tree

PLATFORM VERSION 2

In some cases, such as a low branch near the platform, you will want to extend the 2 × 6 frame boards to move the platform away from the tree.

Shimmed platform without the 2 × 6 extensions

If the tree trunk is branch-free at platform height and another 4 feet above, the edge of the platform will touch the trunk and the long 2 × 6 frame boards will not need to be extended.

However, if there are branches in the way, you must extend the 2 × 6 frame boards to move the platform far enough away from the trunk. You may also add a length of 2 × 4 to act as a shim to hold the platform away from the trunk. This provides some clearance for the roof overhang.

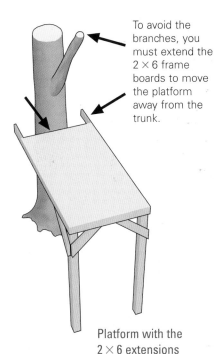

To avoid the branches, you must extend the 2 × 6 frame boards to move the platform away from the trunk.

Platform with the 2 × 6 extensions

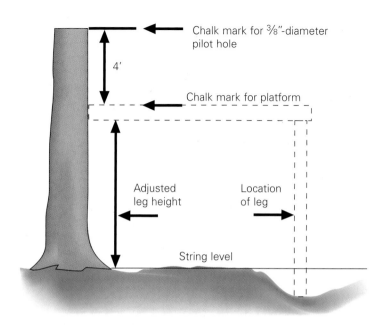

Plan for making chalk marks

It is always better to do as much building as possible on the ground, rather than working on a ladder or up in a tree. So leave the platform upside down in your driveway, and go to the host tree with your ladder, a long tape measure, some chalk, and your cordless drill, with which you will drill a ⅜-inch pilot hole. Measure the trunk from the ground to the height of the platform legs, and make a chalk mark on the trunk. Measure up 4 feet more, and make another mark. Drill a 4-inch-deep pilot hole at this point directly above the place on the trunk where the rear of the platform will touch. Note that the ground may slope away from the tree. Use a small stake, string, and a string level to determine the adjustment.

In either case, adjust the first chalk mark up or down to account for the difference. Note that this is not a critical measurement. The cable length can be adjusted during installation.

Return to the platform with your drill. You will also need three $4 \times \frac{1}{2}$-inch galvanized lag screws with large washers, 10 feet or more of $\frac{3}{16}$-inch, 840-pound test working-load cable, five matched cable clamps, and three matched thimbles. Clamps and thimbles are sized for particular-size cables.

You must now prepare the cable that will support the legless end of the platform. Do not cut the cable yet. Refer to the diagram below, at right, and loop the cable around a thimble, as shown. The cable end should extend 4 or 5 inches, to allow room for the clamps. Put one clamp on loosely, slide it up snug to the thimble, and then tighten the nuts. (A thin-walled socket works best.) Hold the clamp body with vise grips to provide leverage as you tighten.

Apply a second clamp, and your loop is complete. Note that in this instance the raw cable end does not have to be taped because it will be located out of reach behind the house.

JUST WHAT DOES 840-POUND WORKING LOAD MEAN, AND HOW IS IT DETERMINED?

In one of the many thousands of government facilities, there are people with machines and instruments. Here is what they do with galvanized cable, for instance. They mount a sample to a machine that will stretch the cable until it breaks and record the effort to do so. They do this many times using samples from different reels. They then determine the average breaking point—in this case, 4,200 pounds. Twenty percent of that amount (840 pounds) determines the test, or working load. The safety factor is quite generous.

In engineering terms, this stretching force is called stress. These are the forces you will encounter.

Stress = Stretching
Compression = Squeezing
Bending = What you do to a twig to snap it
Torque = Twisting
Shearing = Chopping

Cable loop

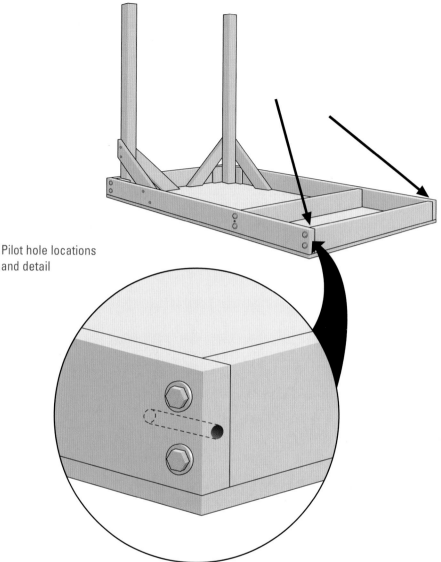

Pilot hole locations
and detail

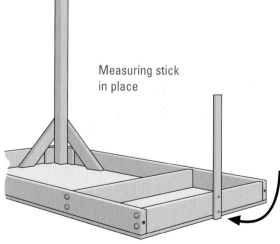

Measuring stick
in place

Drill one ⅜-inch × 4-inch-deep pilot hole into the end of each of the long 2 × 6s (the end opposite the legs).

Cut a 5-foot length of scrap lumber for use as a measuring stick. Place the measuring stick vertically on the ground at the exact center of the platform at the rear. Although you are fabricating this upside down for convenience, you must trust me that the cable length will be correct.

Insert one deck screw through the measuring stick and into the frame, check for vertical, and insert a second screw, to hold the stick securely while you work.

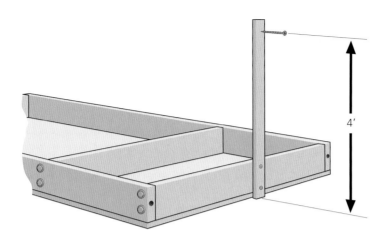

Measuring to place one deck screw

Measure up 4 feet from the ground, and insert a long deck screw partway.

Now feed a lag screw and washer through the cable loop you just made, and crank the screw into either of the pilot holes. It should be snug but not so tight that the thimble can't rotate. Drape the cable over the screw at the top of the vertical stick, and hold it on the remaining empty pilot hole. (Do not take up the slack.) Cut the cable 12 inches past the pilot hole, as shown below.

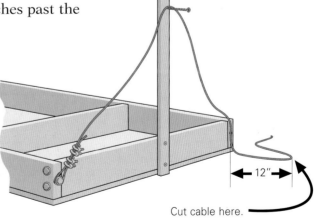

Cut cable here.

Cable in position to be cut

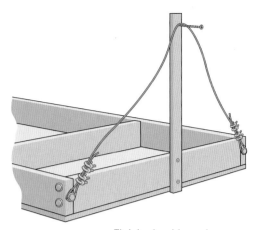

Finished cable ends

Put a washer and a thimble on a lag screw, and screw it into the second pilot hole halfway.

Without taking up the slack, wrap the cable around the thimble and apply two clamps.

When finished, it should look like the drawing at left.

Put a thimble on the deck screw on top of the vertical board. Lay the cable in the thimble groove; then pinch the cable evenly together below the thimble and apply one clamp. This keeps the cable from slipping from side to side when in use.

It is assumed that you have already attached the two legs. If not, screw them on, as described on pages 40–43.

Find someone young and strong to help you move your finished platform to the tree. Turn it upright, and lean the back against the trunk a bit high, as shown here.

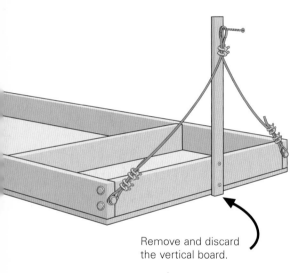

Remove and discard
the vertical board.

Finished cable center

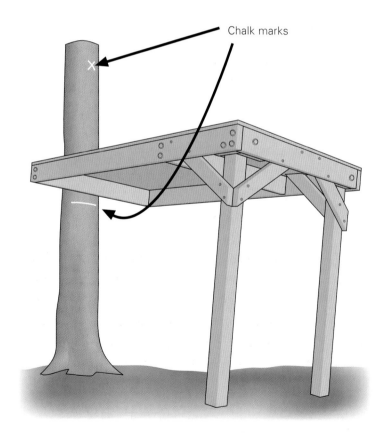

Chalk marks

Using chalk marks

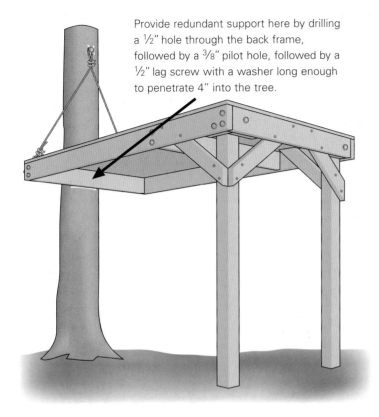

Provide redundant support here by drilling a ½" hole through the back frame, followed by a ⅜" pilot hole, followed by a ½" lag screw with a washer long enough to penetrate 4" into the tree.

Cable installed

Take your third lag screw and washer and a wrench, climb up your firmly positioned ladder, feed the lag screw with washer through the middle thimble on the cable, and crank it into the pilot hole in the trunk. It should be snug but not tight.

Remove the ladder. You and your helper must now slowly pick up the two legs and move away from the tree until the back of the platform no longer touches the trunk. At this point, the cable takes half the load. Move back toward the tree until the platform back just touches the trunk, and lower the legs. Check to see whether either leg needs shimming. Put a level on the platform top, and check both ways. Close is good enough.

This version is finished.

CHAPTER 7

THE PLATFORM in TWO TREES

A platform hung between two trees is our Version 3. In addition to cable supports, this platform is also anchored directly to one of the trees. This is a satisfying configuration, because the house is supported completely by the trees. If you have two sturdy trees (6 inches in diameter or more) that are 7 to 12 feet apart and branch free in the right places, this will work well for you.

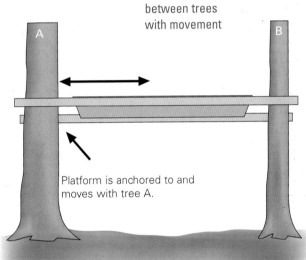

Platform in place between trees with movement

Platform is anchored to and moves with tree A.

PLATFORM VERSION 3

One end of the platform (preferably the back) will be anchored to one of the trees. The decision is yours, as long as the anchor tree is very sturdy.

Assume that the treehouse is anchored to tree A. As tree A sways in the wind, the platform and anything on it will move with the tree trunk. At tree B, the platform is hung like a swing, making the movement of B of no concern. The platform is free to move a bit in any direction in relation to B.

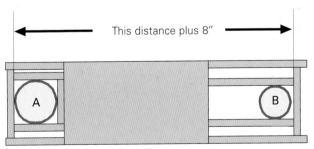

This distance plus 8"

Plan view of tree with platform touching one tree and measuring guideline

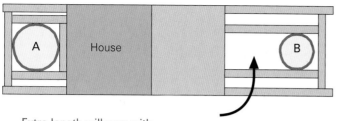

Extra length will vary with specific trees.

This is important because when a good-size tree sways in the wind, the forces are very strong. Side-sway pressure can run well up into the hundreds of pounds.

When measuring the long 2 × 6s for your platform, you will use the distance from the far side of one tree to the far side of the other plus 8 inches.

The reason for the extra length (to be shown later) is that you must provide a redundant support system, which the previous configurations did not require, because the failure of any one part of the other configurations would create significant sag but not a collapse. Here, you must provide double supports at both ends, so that if one support fails, nothing will happen. Note that on the anchor side the diameter of that trunk plus 4 inches determines the beginning of the platform.

The gap at the other side will vary according to the actual distance between your trees.

PLATFORM CONSTRUCTION

The basic construction is the same as that of the other platforms, the only difference being the length of the 2 × 6s.

Your finished platform will look like the illustration at left.

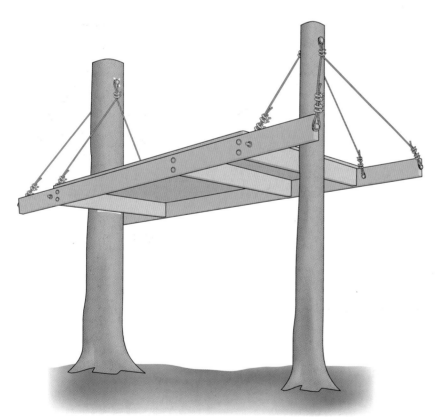

Finished platform

Drill ⅜-inch lag bolts for pilot holes in the ends of the long 2 × 6s. In addition, drill four ½-inch holes through the sides of the same boards. At the anchor side, drill the holes 1 inch from the platform end. At the other end, measure the diameter of that trunk plus 4 inches. Mark and drill on the centerline of the 2 × 6.

You will need four ½ × 3-inch eyebolts, four nuts, and eight washers. Bolt the eyebolts through the center sides, eye to the inside, but leave them loose.

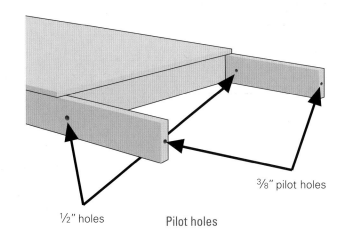

½" holes   Pilot holes   ⅜" pilot holes

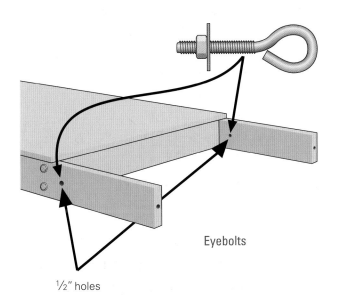

Eyebolts

½" holes

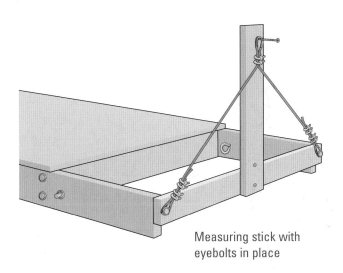

Measuring stick with eyebolts in place

Temporarily screw a scrap 2 × 4 across one end of the long 2 × 6s. Measure and mark the center point of the 2 × 4 between the 2 × 6s.

Screw a 5-foot length of 2 × 4 perpendicular to the marked 2 × 4. Center it on that mark. Measure up 4 feet from the bottom of the marked 2 × 4, and insert a long screw partway.

Now make the support cable as described on pages 47–50. When you are finished, remove the lag screws and make three more cables to that length.

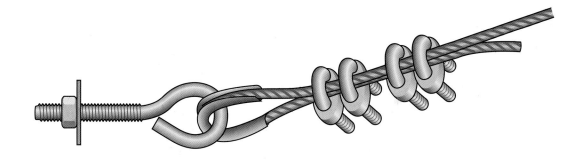

Cable assembly

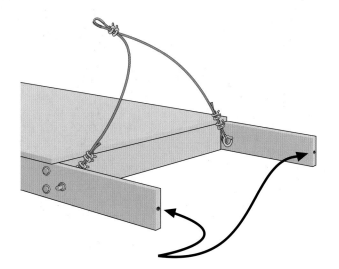

End cables

Keep in mind that two of these cables will be used with the four eyebolts, which means that when you build the cable end loops you must build the loop through the eyebolt.

First, put the thimble on the eyebolt. If necessary, pry the thimble open some to get it on; then vise-grip it back into shape. Feed the cable through the eyebolt, around the thimble, and apply the clamps; then do the same on the other end of the cable. Don't worry if the cable length is off a little. You will make an easy adjustment in the tree. Remember that you need two of these cables.

PREPARING TO ATTACH THE CABLES

Remove the temporary 2 × 4s, and bolt on the two inner cables. Remember, eyes on the inside, and this time draw them up tight.

Do not attach the end cables yet. The platform 2 × 6s must go past each trunk before the end cables can be installed.

Now get some help, move the unit between the host trees, and stand it against one of them, as shown at the top of page 57.

You have by now decided how high the platform will be. Using your extension ladder, measure up to that height plus 4 feet on the platform side of each trunk. Mark and drill a $\frac{3}{8}$ × 3-inch pilot hole.

LIFTING THE PLATFORM

It is assumed here that you wisely did not go beyond 10 or 12 feet in height for your platform, thus eliminating the need for a block-and-tackle hoist. If necessary, get a couple of strong friends to lift the platform a bit while you are up there ready to crank in a lag bolt with a washer. It should be snug, not tight. Make sure your ladder will not interfere with the 2 × 6 ends.

Now move your ladder to the back of the other tree. Have the same two friends lift the other end of the platform using a couple of 2 × 4s so that you can secure the other eyebolt cable.

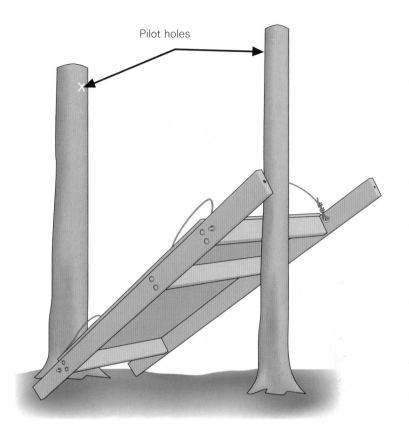

Pilot holes

Lifting position

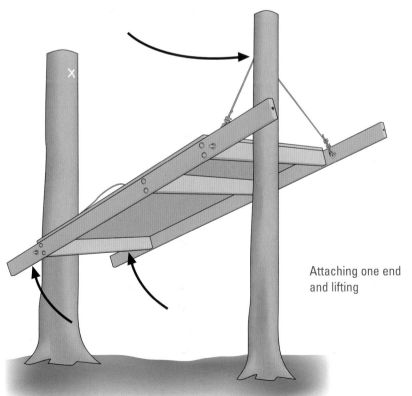

Attaching one end and lifting

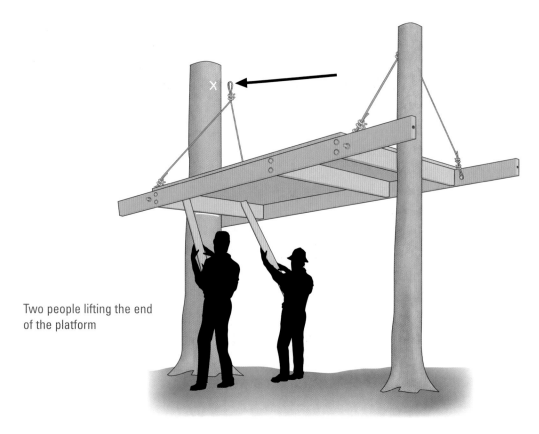

Two people lifting the end
of the platform

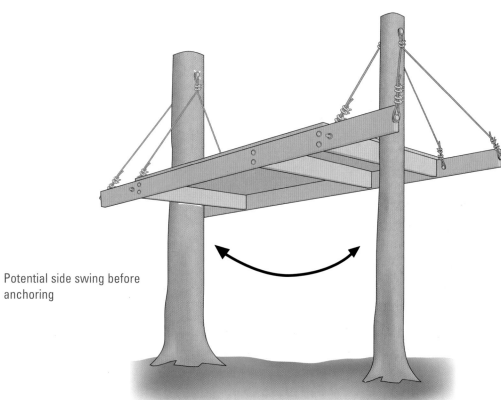

Potential side swing before
anchoring

Check the level tree to tree, not side to side. Close is good enough. If you are off by a significant amount, tie a string to one lag screw and hold it tight (use a string level) near the opposite lag screw. Mark, drill a new pilot hole, and move that lag screw.

Note that now the whole platform behaves like a hammock, swinging side to side, until some part of the platform touches a trunk. It looks like the illustration at the bottom of page 58 when viewed from below.

The platform touches the trunk on the left, and thus prevents it from moving left. You must restrict movement to the right and from side to side. A small movement (up to one inch) is desirable, as it enhances the experience of being up in the trees.

To prevent movement to the right, just add a 45-inch length of 2 × 6 to the left end. You will see that this is the reason for the extra 4 inches added to the extension of the 2 × 6 frame.

Eyeball the position of the new 2 × 6 (leaving a gap of 1 inch or less between the new board and the trunk, to allow for tree growth). Sink two 4-inch deck screws on each side above and below the lag screw pilot hole, as shown at right.

Do the same at the other end of the platform, except that you will leave a full 1-inch space between the trunk and the new 2 × 6.

The reason for this is that this 2 × 6 will not be used to control left-to-right (end-to-end) movement. Only the left side does this.

Next, you will provide control for side-to-side movement. This control is the same on both sides.

Your two new end 2 × 6s were installed by eyeballing, not measuring, which means that they may well be cocked a bit, which is okay.

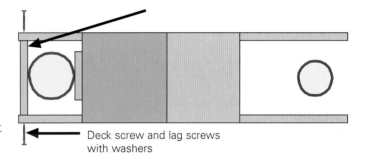

Deck screw and lag screws with washers

New board attached for anchoring

New 2 x 6

1″ gap

Allowing for a 1″ gap

This means that you should measure each side-board piece individually. To do this, lay a 2 × 6 piece on the platform and butt it against the new 2 × 6 end piece. Draw a pencil line on the underside of the 2 × 6 where it meets the platform.

Eyeball in place ¼ inch or less from the trunk, and insert two each 4-inch deck screws in each end. Use the same procedure for the other three boards. Note that as the tree grows, it is easy to adjust any of these boards.

Finally, screw each end cable to the ends of the 2 × 6s. Put a lag screw with a washer through the middle thimble/loop, raise it up as high as you can on the trunk, and give it a tap to mark the spot. Drill a ⅜ × 3-inch pilot hole; then crank the lag bolt in snug but not tight.

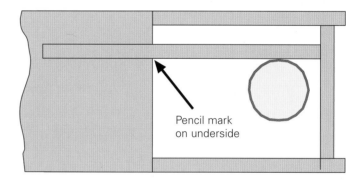

Plan view showing marking for extra side boards

Plan view with four side boards installed

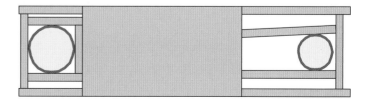

Board at an angle

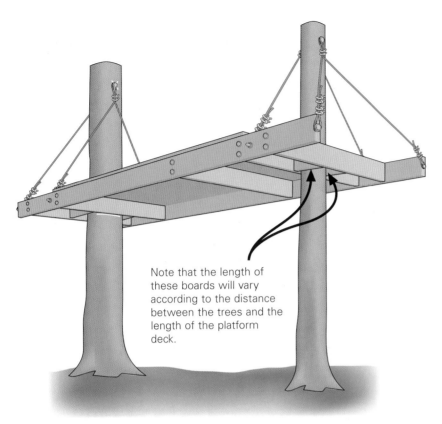

Note that the length of these boards will vary according to the distance between the trees and the length of the platform deck.

Finished platform with new boards in place

This new cable will probably not be taking much of the load, but, in this case, load balance is not necessary.

Your platform is finished. If, in the distant future, a cable should fail, the platform will stay put—even if you are up there relaxing with four of your football linebacker buddies.

You should now climb up there with a lawn chair and have a seat. Try it on for size. Notice how things move a bit when you shift in your chair. Feel the sensation of elevation. Look up at the leaves. Welcome to a new world—you have earned it. Now invite those eager kids to come up too. Maybe one at a time, and only while you are there, since there are no railings to hold on to.

INCREASING THE PORCH

Not meaning to complicate the issue, but an obvious option should be mentioned here.

If your two trees are more than 9 feet apart, you will have some wasted space in front. You could, at completion, apply a piece of the plywood decking on this area and increase the size of your porch.

CHAPTER 8

BUILDING ACCESS to YOUR TREEHOUSE

Now that you have a platform 10 or 12 feet in the air, you have some things to consider. You should be concerned about unauthorized visitors. That is a hazard not to be taken lightly. A policy of no access without adult supervision is by far the best. And it is hoped that your chosen spot is in full view of the kitchen window. A removable set of steps is your best security.

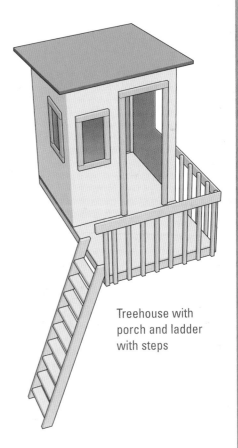

Treehouse with porch and ladder with steps

LADDER STEPS

The recommendation here is a one-piece, lightweight, removable set of steps. A rope or rope-and-rod ladder is not recommended. These have to be anchored at the top and bottom and can be difficult for young people to climb.

A regular long ladder would be suitable, but experience has shown, with the ladder in the photo at left, that above 6 feet the very young and their moms get nervous. Even though the angle is quite steep, they negotiate steps very well using hands and feet.

This is how you build a ladder with steps:

Lean a long 1 × 6 length of decking lumber (your first stringer) on edge against the part of the platform where the ladder will rest when completed. The 1 × 6 should top the platform by at least 6 inches. Adjust it to the angle you like.

NAMES OF PARTS 🏠

Here is a side view of some stairs. You should know the names of the parts you will be making.

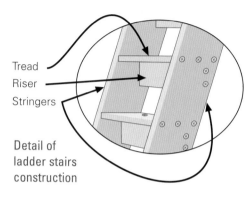

Tread
Riser
Stringers

Detail of ladder stairs construction

As you can see, there are three basic parts: tread (step), riser, and stringer. The stringer is a long board used on both sides of the stairs that holds everything together. A riser is a vertical board that provides bracing and, in many cases, has a cosmetic function. The tread is a board that you tread (or step) on. (The terms "step," "riser," and "stringer" are used in the plans.)

Try 30 degrees from vertical. Drive a small stake into the ground where the 1 × 6 touches it.

Take your level and draw a pencil line, as shown in the bottom illustration.

Clamp or screw the stringer evenly to another 1 × 6 stringer of the same length. (Stairs have two sides.) Cut both stringers at the same time along the pencil line.

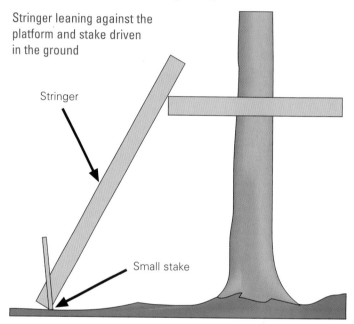

Stringer leaning against the platform and stake driven in the ground

Stringer

Small stake

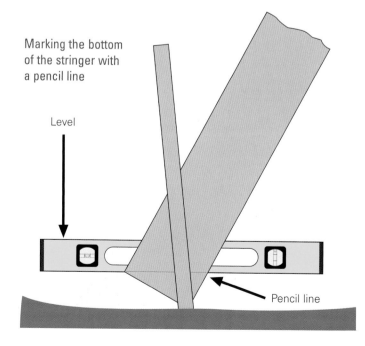

Marking the bottom of the stringer with a pencil line

Level

Pencil line

Place both stringers back in position, still clamped together, as shown below.

The cut face of the stringers should rest flat on the ground as they lean against the platform. Lay your level or any straight board flat on the platform top extending out along-side the two clamped stringers, and make another pencil line, as shown in the bottom illustration.

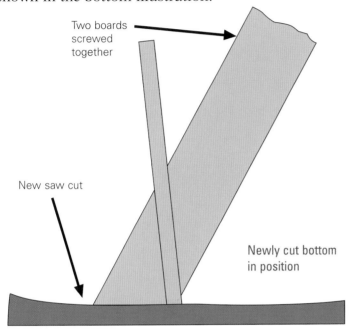

Two boards screwed together

New saw cut

Newly cut bottom in position

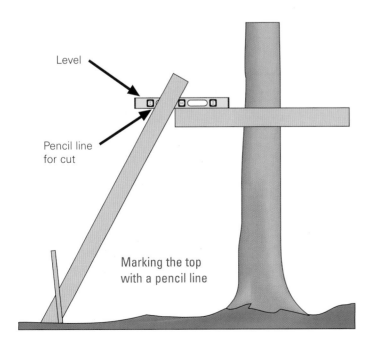

Level

Pencil line for cut

Marking the top with a pencil line

Do not cut at this time. Leave the stringers where they are, and measure the distance in inches from the top of the platform to the ground. You need to know the vertical distance from the platform top to a point directly below that is level with the spot on which the stringer bottom ends rest.

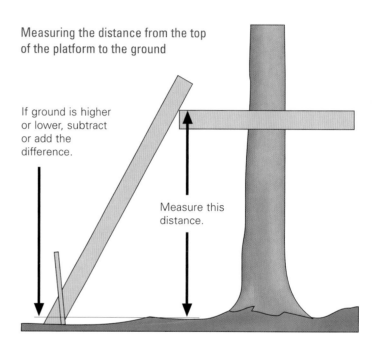

Measuring the distance from the top of the platform to the ground

If ground is higher or lower, subtract or add the difference.

Measure this distance.

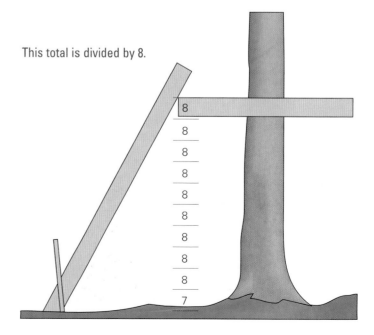

This total is divided by 8.

8
8
8
8
8
8
8
8
8
7

If the ground slopes up or down, as shown on page 66 at top, a good eyeball estimate will do. Add or subtract the amount of slope.

Divide this total by 8. If the remainder is 2 inches or less, use 8 inches as your riser elevation. If the remainder is more, try 7½ or 7 inches.

When you determine your riser measurement, start from the pencil line at the very top of the riser.

Measure down that amount, and, using your level, draw a line parallel to the pencil line at the top. Repeat this process all the way down.

From the last step to the ground will most likely not be quite that measure, but no one will notice. Now you must transfer the lines to the other stringer. Leave the stringers clamped and in place; don't measure again—the lower steps will be slanted if you do. Instead, drill a very small hole through each pencil line. Go all the way through both stringers. Take your level and go to the other side of the stringers. Put the level on each drill hole, and draw another line. This will keep things in line and, at the same time, set it up so that when you unclamp the stringers, all you do is switch them right to left and left to right. This way, the

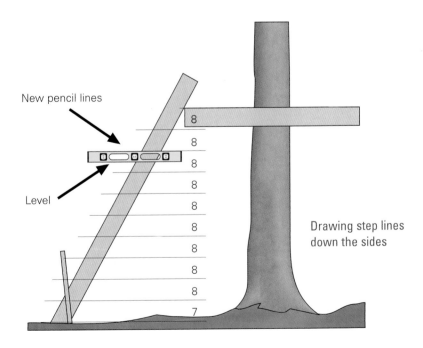

New pencil lines

Level

8
8
8
8
8
8
8
8
8
7

Drawing step lines down the sides

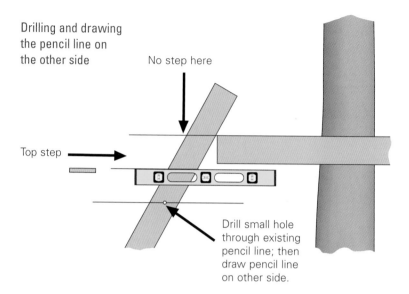

Drilling and drawing the pencil line on the other side

No step here

Top step

Drill small hole through existing pencil line; then draw pencil line on other side.

Stringers on sawhorse

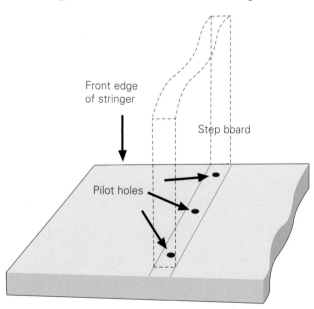

Front edge of stringer

Step board

Pilot holes

Marking the step bottom

pencil lines will be on the inside of each stringer facing one another, where they belong. Note that these pencil lines represent the top of each step, not the top of each riser.

The step boards (made from the same type of lumber used for the sides) should be 16 inches long. Cut the number of steps you need now. The length should be as uniform as possible. At the same time, cut an equal number and length of 1 × 4 exterior lumber. These will be used as bracing and a form of riser.

Now you need to drill ⅛-inch pilot holes for screws to attach the steps to the stringers. Lay the two stringers on your sawhorses, pencil-lines up. Place one of the step boards vertically as shown at upper left. One edge should be on the pencil line, and the other edge should be below, as though it was in its assembled position. Draw a pencil line on the lower edge. This helps you to find center when drilling.

Do this for all steps on both stringers. (This set of steps has no step at the very top.) These lines are your drilling guides for the pilot holes. Drill three ⅛-inch pilot holes between each set of pencil lines, as shown on page 68 at bottom left. Place one hole centered and the others at 1 inch from each edge.

There is one more task to complete before assembly begins—marking the location of the upright risers/braces.

Take any one of the 1 × 4 risers, and lay it on end on any one of the lines that indicate the bottom of a step. Move it to the back until the bottom of the riser is close to the back edge of the stringer. Hold it perpendicular to the step line, and draw a pencil line around it. Eyeballing is good enough for this step.

Note that the reason it is placed back as far as possible is so that little toes don't hit it.

Now take a piece of poster board or thin cardboard (it must be cut square), lay it on the pencil lines, as shown (below at center), and make a mark where indicated.

Simply lay the poster board on all of the other lower step lines on that one stringer, lining it up using the mark, and

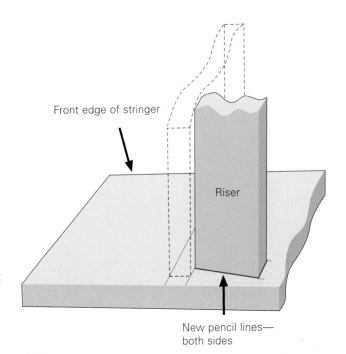

Marking for the riser

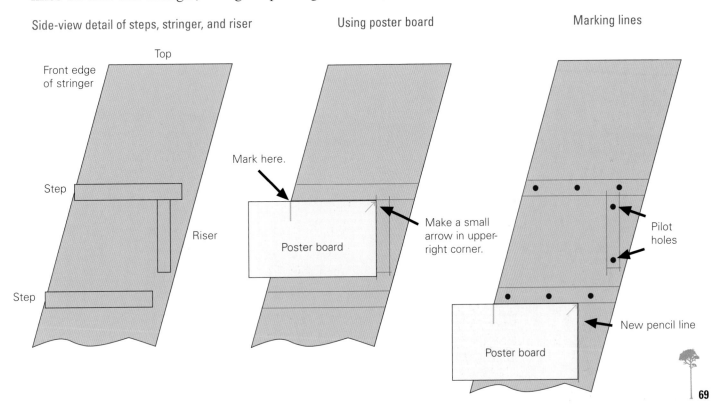

Side-view detail of steps, stringer, and riser

Using poster board

Marking lines

69

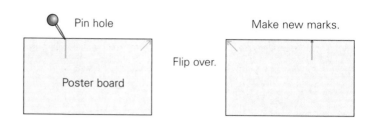

Transferring to the other side for mirror-image use

Pin hole

Poster board

Flip over.

Make new marks.

draw a pencil line, as shown on page 69, bottom right. Do not mark the other stringer at this time.

Pick up the 1 × 4 riser, line it up with the new pencil line, and draw a new line on the other side (the right). This is your pilot hole drilling guide for the riser. Drill two ⅛-inch pilot holes between the pencil lines 1 inch down from the top edge and 1 inch up from the bottom edge of the riser. Do this for all riser locations on that one stringer.

The other stringer is a mirror image of the one just completed. Take a pin and poke a hole through the poster board where you marked it; then flip it over and make a new mark over the pinhole. You now have a mirror-image template for the other stringer. Repeat the process for the remaining pilot holes.

Lay the stringers on a flat surface, as shown at left, with pencil lines up.

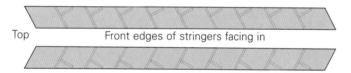

Top

Front edges of stringers facing in

Stringer positions

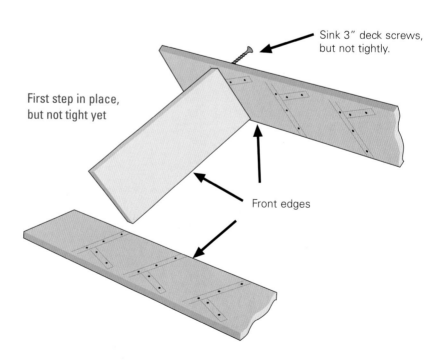

Sink 3" deck screws, but not tightly.

First step in place, but not tight yet

Front edges

Start at the top of one stringer, with your screws in your apron pocket and your drill with the proper screw bit handy.

Note that the stringer is in effect standing front-edge down. As you line up each step on the angled pencil lines, you should rest the edge of the step flat on the ground or working surface. This will make the front edge of all steps line up evenly with the front edge of the stringers.

Feed screws into the pilot holes for the first step. Place a step carefully on the ground and then the lines, and sink the screws, but not tight. Next, raise the other stringer on edge, line up the step with the lines on the new stringer, and insert three screws loosely. It will now be self-supporting.

At this point, you can screw the rest of the steps into the first stringer—tightly. Then screw in all of the riser braces into the first stringer—tightly. Be sure to hold the stringers tightly to the step above. If you have cut everything square and to exactly the same length, you will experience no fitting problems.

Go to the other stringer and line up. Loosely screw in the step next to the one already installed, and work your way to the other end.

Now go back and screw in the risers—holding them tight to the steps above.

Now tighten all screws in no particular order.

You should now sink three screws, spaced evenly, down through each step into the riser brace.

The steps are now complete, except for attaching the handy 4-inch bicycle hooks at the top.

When the hooks are on the ladder, set it in place and mark where the hook ends touch the platform top. Remove the ladder, and drill two holes in the platform to accept the hooks.

Note that when this ladder is used, the climber should perform a near vertical crawl going up and assume the same position going down.

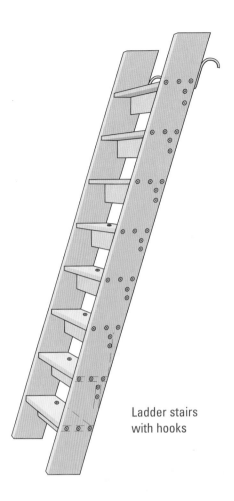

Ladder stairs with hooks

Close-up of hook

CHAPTER 9

THE HOUSE

Plans for a basic house are presented here. As you gain experience, these building techniques can be greatly modified to suit unique situations. The basics are the same. Parts of the house may seem somewhat flimsy as you work on them on the ground, but when the house is attached to the platform in the tree, it becomes a stable, secure structure.

BASIC HOUSE STRUCTURE

First, look at a plain box, built without doors or windows, to get a clear understanding of the basic parts of the structure. See "House Material" on page 27 in Chapter 3 for the required materials.

You can see that once the sides are screwed to the front and back, it becomes a strong, framed box. Since this house is a 4 × 4-foot square box, no further framing is necessary.

The height of this house is a compromise that will accommodate most users. The front is 5½ feet tall, sloping to 5 feet at

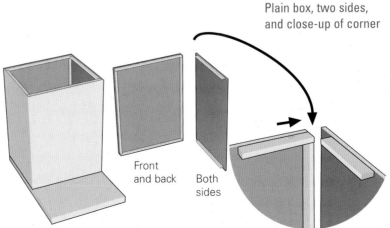

Plain box, two sides, and close-up of corner

Front and back   Both sides

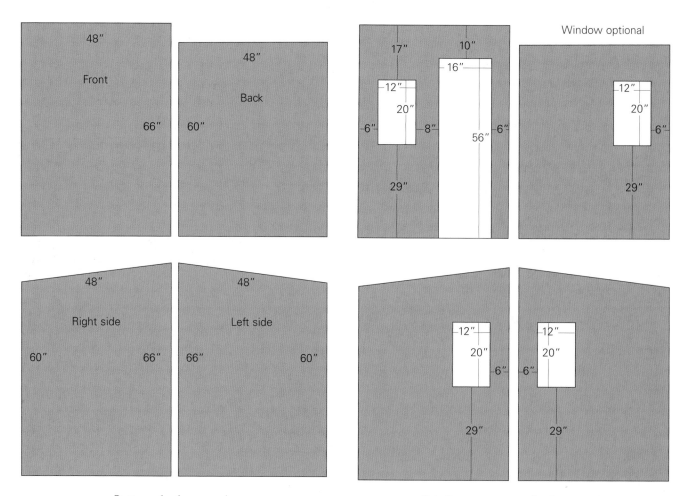

| Patterns for four panels | Detail measurements for four panels |

Within the diagram:

Front — 48", 66"

Back — 48", 60"

Right side — 48", 60", 66"

Left side — 48", 66", 60"

Window optional

17", 10", 16", 12", 20", 6", 8", 56", 6", 29", 12", 20", 6", 29"

12", 20", 6", 6", 12", 20", 29", 29"

the back. It is a comfortable height for most children. In a child's house, the ceiling should be child size and adult visitors can bend a bit. The door is 16 inches wide × 56 inches high. Again, this is child size but manageable for adults. Window sizes are optional, but keep in mind that a tiny window is cute and a large window must incorporate something to prevent a child from using it as an exit.

Start by cutting the four walls from four sheets of ¼-inch exterior 4 × 8-foot plywood. (Exterior is best, of course, but regular will do if you paint it well.)

If your plywood is the good-on-one-side type and you want to have the smooth side on the inside, remember to cut the side pieces as mirror images.

Now pencil in the cut lines for the door and window(s). Note that a right-side door is shown here. A mirror image may work well, but read through this section to learn of other considerations.

You may, of course, reposition the door and/or the window(s) as you wish. When the door is penciled in, cut each side up from the bottom approximately 5 inches, but only 5 inches. The rest of the door will be cut out later.

At right is a drawing of the inside front and one side to give you an idea of what you will be building next.

For the frame, use 2 × 3 untreated pine. You don't need a tape measure for this—just a pencil. For comfort while working, you might want to set out your sawhorses and lay three or four straight 2 × 4s on them as a working surface. First, lay a length of 2 × 3 framing lumber on the 2 × 4s, narrow side up; then lay the inside top edge of the plywood front on top of the 2 × 3, as shown below, right (the pencil lines must be up).

One end of the 2 × 3 lines up with the one side edge of the plywood. Draw a pencil line at the opposite edge and cut. (Note that waterproof gluing is okay if you are sure the parts are positioned properly and will never have to be disassembled.) The 2 × 3 will be attached ¼ inch below the top edge.

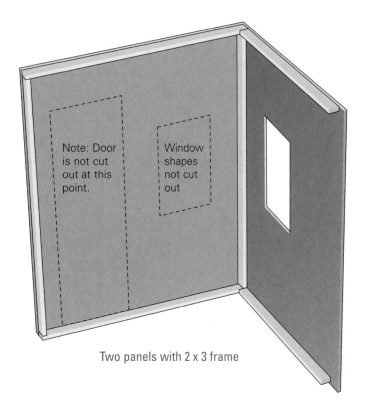

Note: Door is not cut out at this point.

Window shapes not cut out

Two panels with 2 x 3 frame

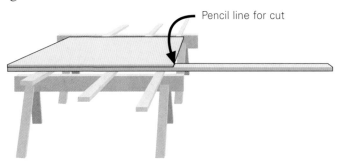

Pencil line for cut

Measuring method

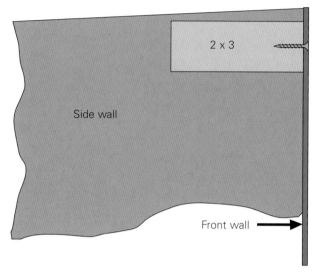

Detail for attaching 2 x 3 frame

The drawing above shows how this is an allowance for the roof slope.

Attach the newly cut 2 × 3 (narrow side) to the plywood using 1½-inch deck screws. Next, measure, mark, and cut the bottom 2 × 3 the same way you did the top. The bottom piece, however, is attached right at the bottom of the plywood. Do not screw the plywood to that portion of the 2 × 3 between the saw cuts for the door. After the front wall is installed on the platform, the portion of the 2 × 3 in the doorway will be cut away. In the meantime, it helps keep things firm and in line.

Now that the top and bottom 2 × 3s are in place, turn the whole assembly over and measure the side, or vertical, 2 × 3s. Use the butt-and-cut method, as shown in the drawing at left.

Measure each side individually (there will be slight differences), and mark the cut 2 × 3s so that you don't mix them up. Screw them in place on each edge of the plywood. A close fit is good enough.

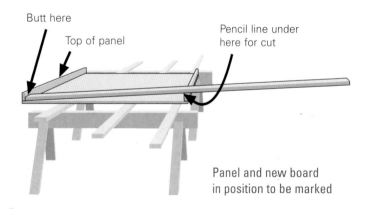

Butt here

Top of panel

Pencil line under here for cut

Panel and new board in position to be marked

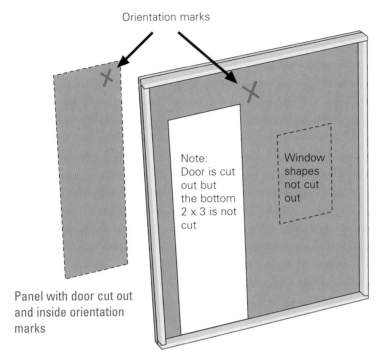

Orientation marks

Note:
Door is cut
out but
the bottom
2 x 3 is not
cut

Window
shapes
not cut
out

Panel with door cut out
and inside orientation
marks

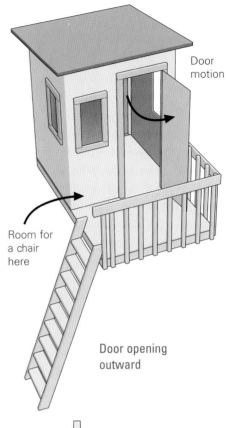

Door
motion

Room for
a chair
here

Door opening
outward

Now that the four frame 2 x 3s are attached to the plywood front, cut out the door. Be as accurate as you can. Save the piece you cut out—it is the door. Be sure to mark the top outside of the door to keep it oriented properly.

Turn the plywood front panel over. It will look like the illustration at top left.

This door will be set up to open outward. A door opening inward decreases usable interior space, and space here is already at a premium. It is best to locate the door on either side of the structure. A door in the middle could work, but the users will forever complain that the space behind the open door is too small for anything.

Next, frame the door on the inside with 1 × 3 strapping lumber. Measure and cut two vertical lengths, as shown, using the butt-and-cut method. Screw from the plywood front into the strapping. Be sure to use short screws that won't stick out the other side where the children will be.

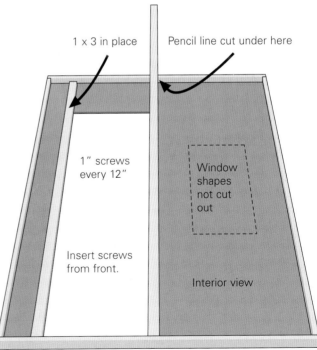

1 x 3 in place

Pencil line cut under here

1" screws
every 12"

Window
shapes
not cut
out

Insert screws
from front.

Interior view

Measuring for the door frame

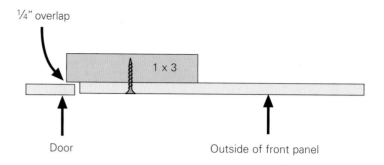

¼" overlap

1 x 3

Door   Outside of front panel

Allowing for overlap

It is very important for the two new boards to overlap the plywood cut lines by ¼ inch. This is so that when the door is closed, it will nest in the plywood cutout and rest against the strapping boards, which means that when closed it stops at the proper place. In addition, this tends to seal out light, wind, and bugs.

When the vertical boards are in place, cut (butt-and-cut) a short strapping board across the top. This also overlaps the door cutout by ¼ inch.

Lay the panel outside up, and cut out the window shape. Follow the lines as closely as you can. Keep in mind that what you are doing here is not fine, precise carpentry, nor

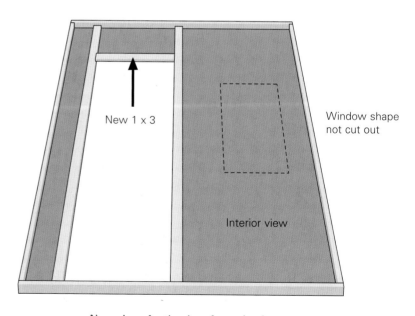

New 1 x 3

Window shape not cut out

Interior view

New piece for the door frame in place

should it be, unless you enjoy the extra work—if so, by all means have fun. Your finished outside window frame will look like the illustration at right. The inner edges on the frame pieces are flush with the cut line of the plywood.

First, lay a piece longer than you need on the bottom of the cutout. Clamp it lightly and check for level. Tighten the clamp, if it is the kind that can be tightened.

Lay a second piece perpendicular to the first piece, and make two marks, as indicated.

Move the new piece to the other side, and make another mark, as indicated.

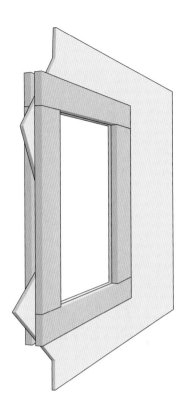

Window frame front view
and cross section

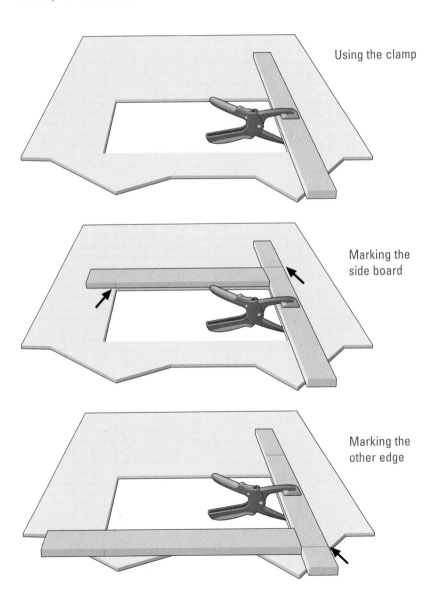

Using the clamp

Marking the
side board

Marking the
other edge

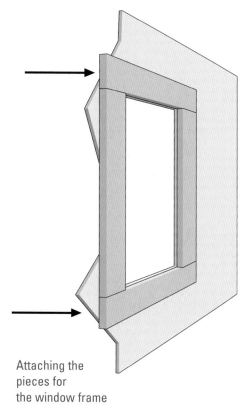

Attaching the
pieces for
the window frame

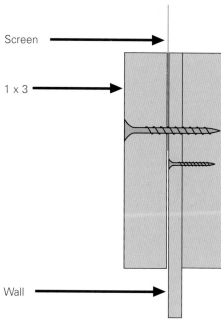

Screen

1 x 3

Wall

Detail for 1 x 3 frame, screen,
and screws

Now remove the horizontal piece and the vertical piece. Measure and cut the pieces to size. You will need four of each piece: two of each for the outside and two of each for the inside.

First, install the bottom piece. Lay it in place using the marks as guides; then turn the panel over and secure it with two small screws.

Turn the panel back over, clamp the remaining pieces in place, and turn over and screw in each piece with two screws each.

When the outside is finished, turn the panel over and get ready to do the same for the inside. But before you attach the pieces, cut a piece of window screen (aluminum is best) 2 inches wider and 2 inches higher than the window opening in the plywood. Staple it in place just enough to hold it.

Now go ahead and attach the inside frame pieces, which, in the process, will clamp the screen in place. Use screws long enough to reach into the outer frame but not through it. Try ¾-inch screws.

The window is complete. Using the same procedure, you may make other windows if you wish.

Leave the front panel lying face up, and fetch the piece of plywood you cut out for the door. Trim ½ inch from the bottom so that the door will open easily. (Check the mark you made on the front top to be sure that you cut the right end.) Next, for strength, make a frame around the outside front of the door using the 1 × 3 strapping lumber. Use short screws from the plywood side.

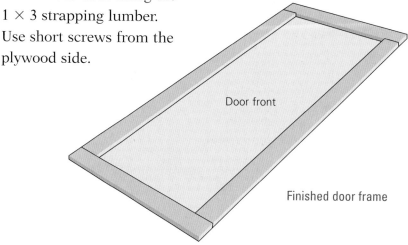

Door front

Finished door frame

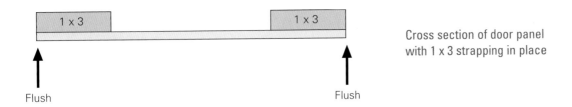

Cross section of door panel
with 1 x 3 strapping in place

1 x 3   1 x 3

Flush   Flush

The outer edges of the door frame should be flush with the edges of the plywood door panel.

Measure and cut the same as you did for the front panel. Cut and attach the top and bottom first. Use ¾-inch screws every 6 inches from the plywood side.

If the 1 × 3 piece covers your mark on the top, make a new mark. Make the verticals using the butt-and-cut method.

The door is ready to be hinged to the front of the house. Be sure to follow the next few steps carefully to ensure that the door will operate smoothly.

Remember that when you cut out the door, probably with your jigsaw, you were careful to cut as straight as possible. Yet, if you look closely, you will see that there are slight irregularities. The drawing here is an exaggerated example.

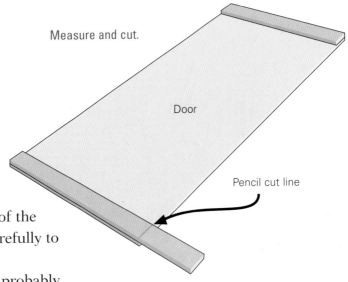

Measure and cut.

Door

Pencil cut line

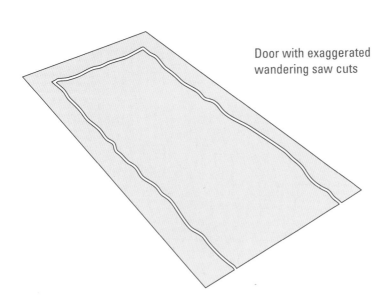

Door with exaggerated
wandering saw cuts

Door must fit to its original position

You can see that, as with a jigsaw puzzle, if the piece is removed, it can properly fit back in only one way. That is the reason you marked the top front. In addition, notice that as you cut, your jigsaw blade removed approximately $\frac{1}{16}$ inch of wood.

When closed, your door must sink back into the large hole. If it doesn't, you must shave one edge or the other. Therefore, when you position the door to put on the hinges, you must center it as closely as possible between the cut lines. In other words, the plywood of the door should be in the same position relative to the front panel as it was before it was cut out. It may seem as though this is excessively stressed, but making a proper door is worth the effort.

Back to work. Before you lay the door in position on the plywood front panel, make three spacers from wood scrap or cardboard. These will be $\frac{1}{2}$ inch wide by $\frac{1}{16}$ inch thick by approximately 2 inches. They often can be made from the cardboard backing of a notepad. Place one spacer on edge on the top edge of the door cutout and two more on the hinge side, as shown.

Door opening showing proper location and position of shims

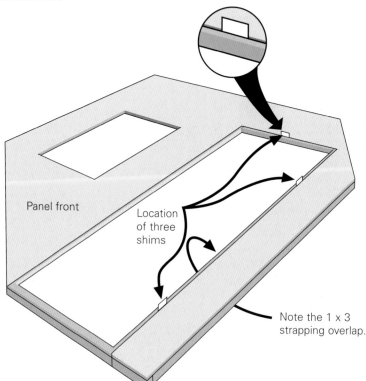

Panel front

Location of three shims

Note the 1 x 3 strapping overlap.

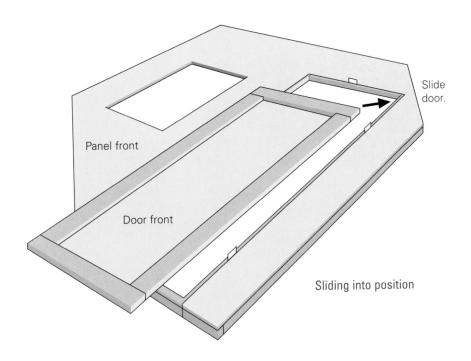

Panel front

Door front

Slide
door.

Sliding into position

Carefully slide the door in place, and push it firmly up and to the side against the three spacers.

When this is done, check the gap on the other long side. Almost touching is okay. Up to a ⅛-inch gap is also okay. Odds are that your door passes this test. If not, you must adjust the thickness of the three spacers.

Once the door is in position and before the hinges can be installed, it is necessary to build a second frame. This one will be on the plywood front around the door opening.

First, without disturbing the door, lay an overlong piece of 1 × 3 above and ¼ inch away from the top of the door. Temporarily hold it in place with two screws inserted into the 1 × 3 and through the plywood.

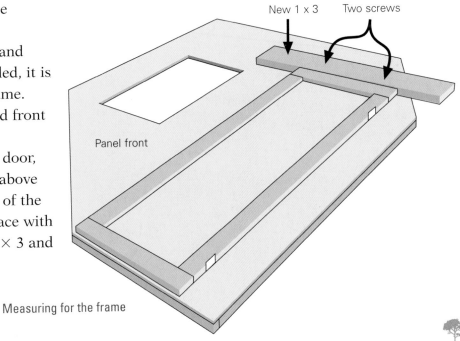

New 1 x 3   Two screws

Panel front

Measuring for the frame

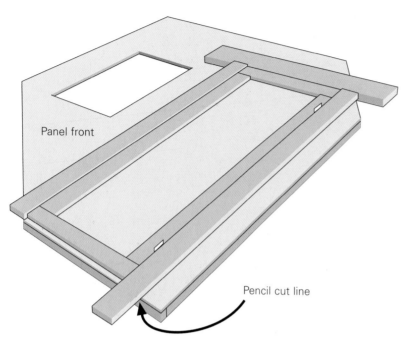

Panel front

Pencil cut line

Measuring the side frame

Butt a new 1 × 3 side piece to the new top piece on either side. Draw a pencil line at the bottom of the plywood and cut two each.

Line up one of the new 1 × 3s with the same ¼-inch gap from top to bottom, and temporarily attach it with two screws. Do the same on the other side with the other vertical piece.

Next, mark the top piece, as shown below, remove the screws, cut off the ends, and screw it back in position.

Remove the door and the three spacers. Turn the front panel over, and screw the new frame in place with short screws. Make sure they do not penetrate all the way through.

Turn the front panel back over, remove the temporary screws from the new frame, replace the three spacers, and reposition the door, as you did before.

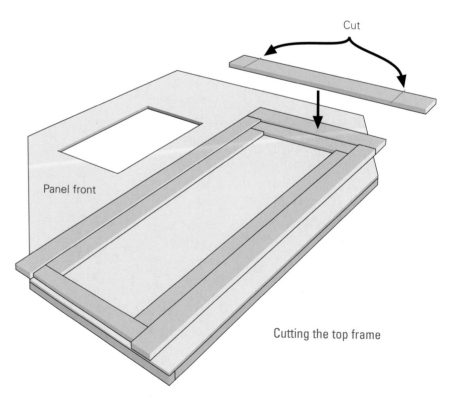

Cut

Panel front

Cutting the top frame

Go get the hinges, which should be flat pin hinges. The size should be approximately as shown at right, but once again close is good enough.

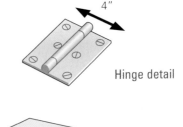

Hinge detail

Mount the hinges as shown approximately 6 inches from the top and bottom. The pin of the hinge should line up with the ¼-inch gap.

Just a reminder, as you work happily along, intent on what you are doing, you just might put the hinges on the wrong side. You can believe this has been done before. Be especially careful if the door you are installing is a mirror image of the one shown here.

Once a hinge is lined up (use masking tape if it helps), use a center punch on one hole (or a nail if that's all you have) and sink a 1¼-inch deck screw halfway.

Now punch and sink another screw partway on the other side.

Slowly finish sinking either screw. Watch to see that on the last turn the hinge does not shift. Do the same to the other screw, and check to make sure the points do not penetrate all the way through. If all is well, punch and drill the remaining four screws in any order.

If you see the hinge shift out of alignment while tightening either of the first two screws, simply back out the offending screw, realign the hinge, center-punch the hole next to the

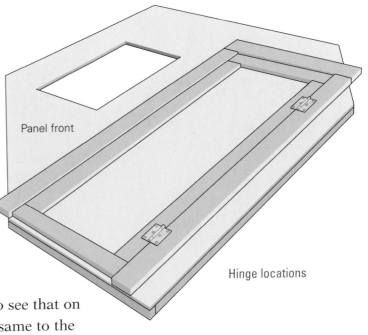

Panel front

Hinge locations

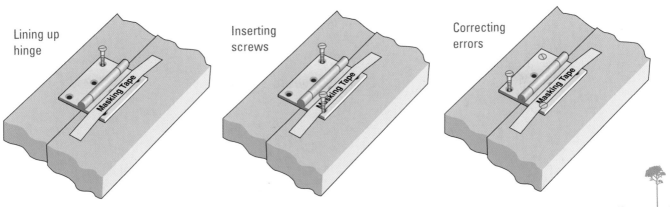

Lining up hinge

Inserting screws

Correcting errors

Masking Tape

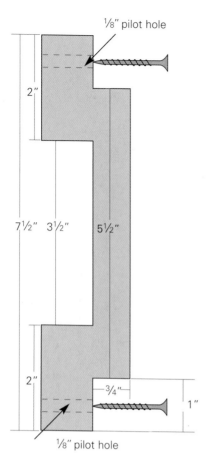

2"

7½" 3½"   5½"

2"

¾"

1"

⅛" pilot hole

Handle pattern details

original screw, and put the screw in the new hole. Finish installing and tightening all of the other screws, and then reinstall the off-center screw in the same hole.

Sure, this is a royal pain, but your reputation is at stake.

When both hinges are in place and secure, lift the handle side of the door to make sure it opens and closes smoothly. In the worst case, you will have to trim a little door plywood.

The door handle is a handle only—it does not incorporate a latch. The solid one-piece handle shown here is made from one piece of 1 × 4 common pine. It is a good size for little hands.

Once you have cut out the handle, sand all edges round, except the surfaces that touch the door frame.

Drill two ⅛-inch pilot holes in the handle as indicated. Place the handle on the door frame at about the middle.

Place the handle back on the door frame, and insert two each 2-inch deck screws from the inside of the door frame.

Insert two 1½-inch deck screws, and you're finished.

This door will not have a latch as such. It will be held closed at all times with a screen-door spring. It is desirable to have a door that remains closed unless someone is passing

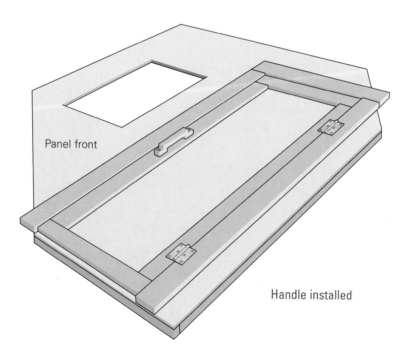

Panel front

Handle installed

through. This feature tends to keep out rain, snow, bees, and small creatures. One squirrel, intent on building a nest, can do an appalling amount of damage. The spring will be installed when the house is assembled in the trees.

The back panel will go quickly. Cut a 4 × 5-foot piece of plywood, and frame it with 2 × 3 lumber. All frame lumber is attached flush to the edges of the plywood. The top piece does not have the ¼-inch space used on the front. Add a window if you wish.

For the sides, cut two mirror-image panels to keep the plywood's good side in. You may make windows. This is recommended, as the windows bring in light. Do not attach any 2 × 3 lumber at this point.

Now you are ready to assemble the sides of the house on the finished platform.

Move all four wall panels to the base of your platform. Lean them neatly against a tree trunk (people are watching). Since these panels are not very heavy, nothing is necessary other than your own hands and arms to raise them to the platform, as needed.

You'll need a cordless drill, an apron pocket full of 1¼-inch deck screws, a hammer (to tap things in place), a few pieces of 1 × 3 scrap, a pocket tape measure, and, of course, a pencil.

First, bring the rear panel to the platform. (Your tools are already there—right?) Stand it upright in its position at the back of the platform.

Note: If your platform is freestanding, the back panel will be mounted flush with the back edge of the platform. This will give you an extra 4 inches of porch space.

If you have either of the other platforms, remember that the tree trunk touches the back of the platform. You must mount the back panel 4 inches in from the back edge of the platform so that the roof overhang in the back does not collide with the trunk of the tree. Or you may shim the platform, as mentioned previously.

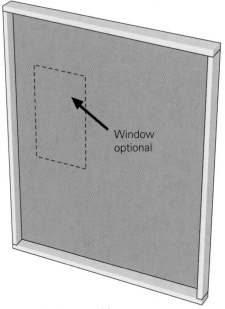

Window optional

Back assembly

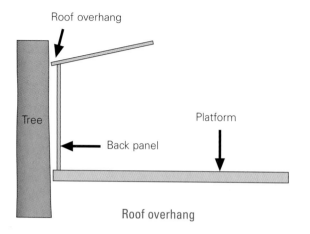

Roof overhang

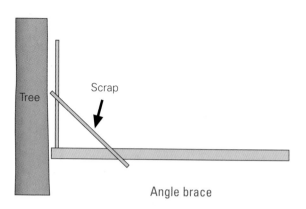

Angle brace

If this is necessary, measure and mark 4 inches in on each side of the platform at the back. Line up the back edge of the back panel with the marks on the platform. It is easiest to have a helper hold the panel in place more or less vertically while you drop a couple of 3-inch deck screws through the 2 × 3 at the bottom of the panel and into the platform. If you don't have a helper, use a scrap 1 × 3 temporary brace, as shown at top right.

Don't check for vertical. The installation of the next panel will take care of this automatically.

What follows is a cross-section drawing of the back panel bottom and the platform. It illustrates the best way to sink the screws that hold the house to the platform.

Position of the back wall

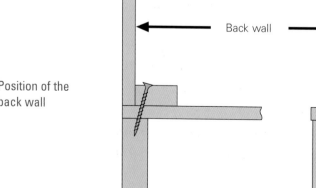

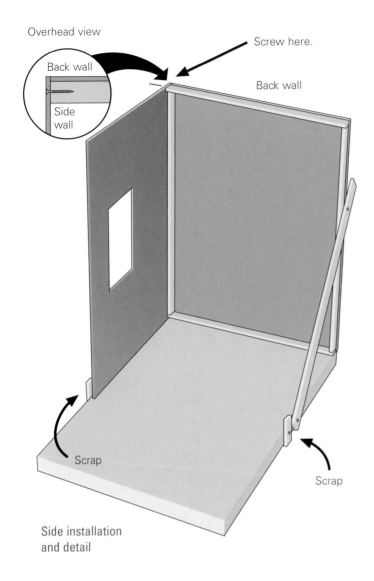

Overhead view

Back wall

Side wall

Screw here.

Back wall

Scrap

Scrap

Side installation
and detail

Now bring up a side panel (either one), hold it in position, as above, and sink one screw in the top corner from the outside.

Notice that the forward bottom of the side panel rests at a slight angle on the platform surface. Should it swing out past the edge of the platform, you can see that it would fall forward and down. You do not want to experience an event like that. The solution is to temporarily screw a scrap on each side to stop each panel from moving out beyond the edge.

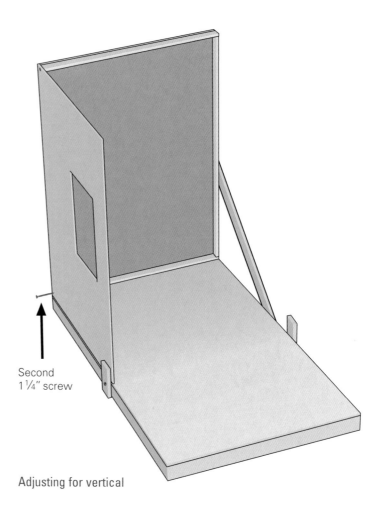

Second
1 $\frac{1}{4}''$ screw

Adjusting for vertical

These scraps can be removed when the sides are fixed to the front panel.

Move to the outside (on your ladder), and sink a screw in the bottom corner of the side panel, as shown above. Be sure to keep the back edge of the side panel lined up with the back of the rear panel.

Do the same for the other side panel.

When that is done, your project will look like the top left illustration on page 91.

It is now time to bring up the front panel. Push the side panels out against the scrap blocks, and slide the front panel in place. Sink a 2-inch deck screw into the top at each side. Tap the bottom in line, and sink two more screws there.

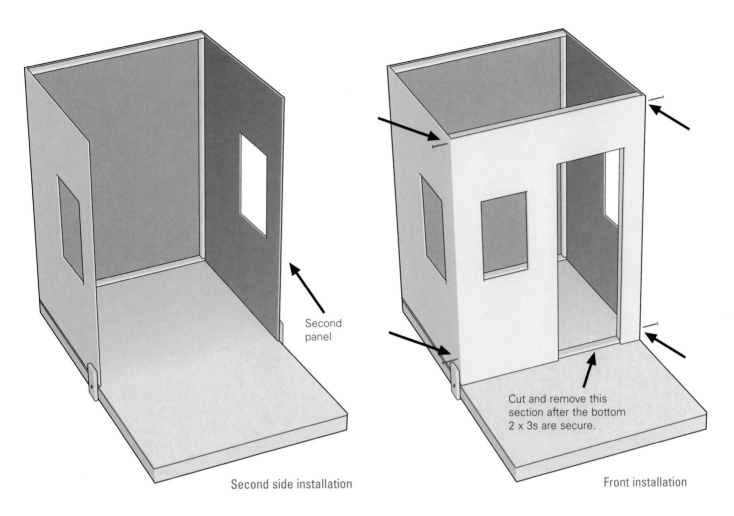

Second panel

Second side installation

Cut and remove this section after the bottom 2 x 3s are secure.

Front installation

Now go back and sink screws every 6 inches up and down each corner. Then step inside the house and sink more 3-inch screws through the bottom 2 × 3s to secure the house to the platform. If there is no 2 × 6 under the platform where a house panel sits, screw up from below with 2-inch deck screws. Note that you must not screw up into the part of the 2 × 3 that runs along the door cutout. As soon as the bottom 2 × 3s have been screwed down tightly, get your handsaw and cut that piece of the 2 × 3 away.

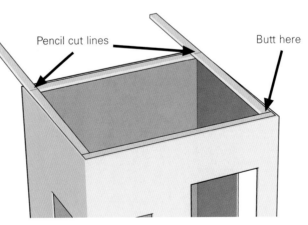

Pencil cut lines

Butt here

Cutting side frame boards

You will need four more lengths of 2 × 3 lumber to finish the side panels. Use butt, mark, and cut for the top pieces on each side. You can angle-cut if you want to, but this is not necessary.

For the bottom two pieces, there is an easy way to measure without using a tape measure. Use two thin strips of wood—in this case, two yardsticks work well. Lay them side to side where the new piece will go. Slide one until it

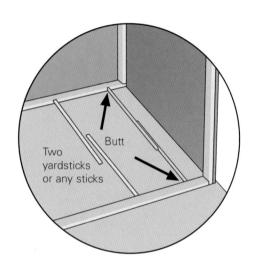

Measuring without numbers

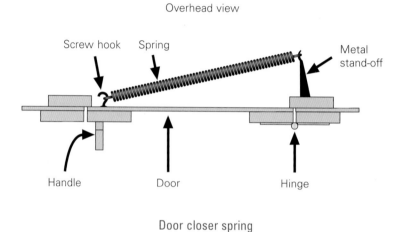

Door closer spring

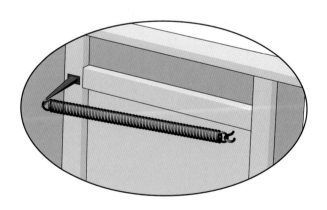

Door closer detail

touches the rear 2 × 3. Slide the other yardstick in the opposite direction until it touches the other 2 × 3. Squeeze them together, and take them to the new 2 × 3 to be cut and make your marks.

Next, you can install the door-closing hardware (available at any hardware store). Just mount close to the top of the door. Follow the diagram in the center of page 92.

Because the roof cannot be cut from one piece of plywood, you need one more 2 × 3 in the middle, as shown below. (Measure for exact center.)

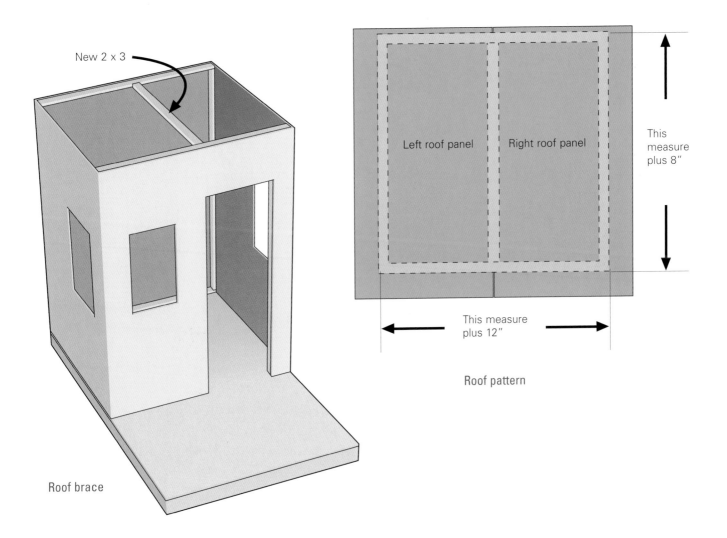

New 2 x 3

Roof brace

Left roof panel

Right roof panel

This measure plus 8"

This measure plus 12"

Roof pattern

Railings

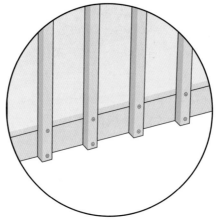

Lower railing detail

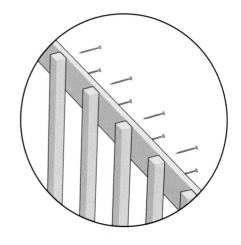

Upper railing detail

Measure the distance from one side panel to the other and add 12 inches, as shown in the drawing on the right on page 93. Divide by 2 to determine the width of each roof panel. Next, measure from the top of the front panel to the top of the rear panel and add 8 inches. This is the length of both roof panels. These measurements provide for a 6-inch overhang for the front and sides and a 2-inch overhang for the back.

Line up the first panel with one edge in the middle of the center 2 × 3. There should be a 6-inch overhang in front and 2 inches in the back. Secure with 1½-inch deck screws every 6 inches. Lay the second panel in place, and sink as many screws as you can reach; then finish the job from your ladder.

Now you need to consider the roof. You may, of course, use any type of shingle, but brushing on fibered roof coating is easiest. The paint and trim are up to you—or maybe the eager child who wants to move in.

You'll also need a railing for your porch.

Use 2 × 2 and 1 × 4 exterior lumber. Cut 32-inch pieces from 8-foot lengths of 2 × 2s. This yields three pieces from each 8-foot length. Screw one every 12 inches along the two edges, as indicated above (center illustration), and double up at the ladder end.

Drill ⅛-inch pilot holes in the 2 × 2s. Use 3-inch screws to attach them to the 2 × 6. Put the 2 × 2 in position and insert one screw. Check for vertical; then sink the other screw. If the points penetrate to the other side of the 2 × 6, that area is well away from little hands. Install all of the 2 × 2s first.

The right-hand illustration on page 94 shows the position of the top rail when attached to the 2 × 2s.

Install the short rail first. Measure from the front edge of one of the front 2 × 2s to 6 inches past the front edge of the house.

Put the 1 × 4 railing in position, and clamp it, as shown below (left).

Check for level, and screw the rail into each 2 × 2 with two each 1½-inch screws. For the place where the railing overlaps the house by 6 inches, cut a 6-inch piece of 2 × 2 and place it between the railing and the house. Screw it to the railing with two each 1½-inch screws, as shown below (center).

Then screw two more 1½-inch screws into this short 2 × 2 from the inside of the house. This makes for a very sturdy railing. Now cut another length of 1 × 4 for the other railing. Measure from the outer edge of the installed railing to 4 inches past the platform edge on the ladder side.

Install it as you did the short railing. At last, your treehouse is finished . . . basically . . . well, almost.

Now you have to think about embellishments, as well as furniture, decorations, devices, and other things.

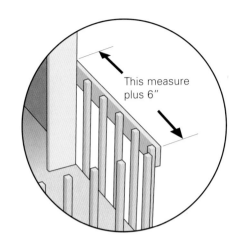

This measure plus 6"

Measuring side rail

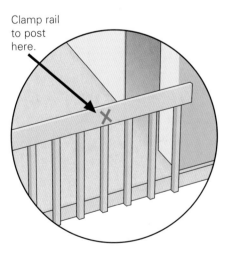

Clamp rail to post here.

Clamping rail to post

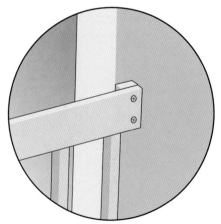

Securing the side rail detail

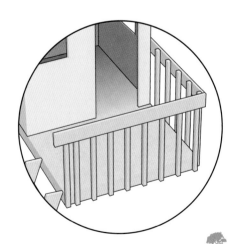

Finished porch

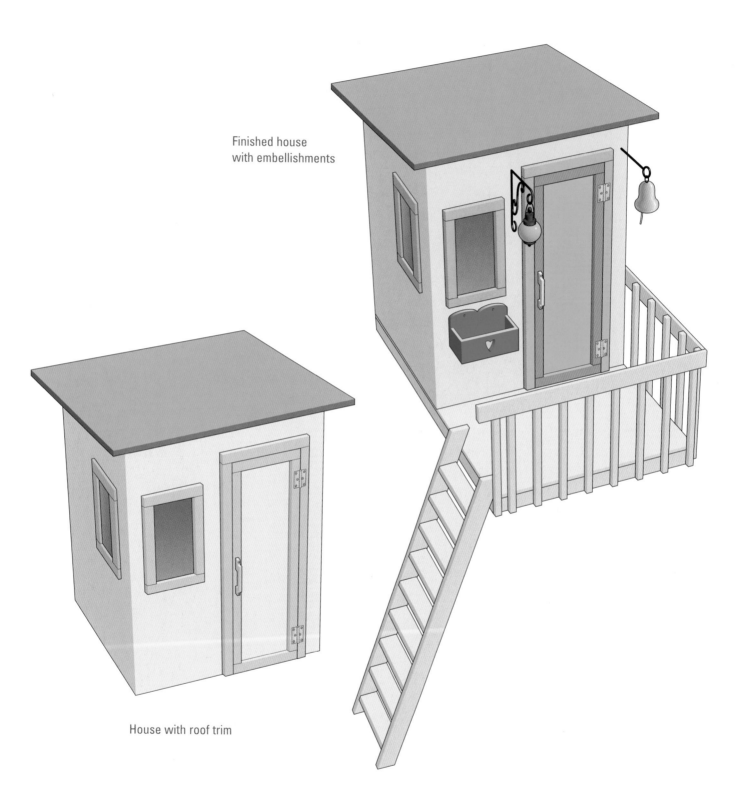

Finished house
with embellishments

House with roof trim

Take a look at the roof line. It is ¼ inch thick—not very substantial. You may want to add 1 × 2 strips of pine to make it look thicker. Just cut strips of the desired thickness, and screw in from the top. The drawing at left on page 96 should be all the direction you need.

Here is a pattern for a simple window box. Use artificial flowers, as soil and water promote decay.

Flower box

Back of box.
Each square = 1"

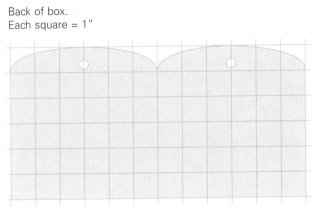

Flower box back pattern

Front of box.
Each square = 1"

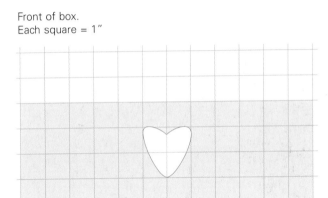

Flower box front pattern

Sides of box.
Each square = 1"

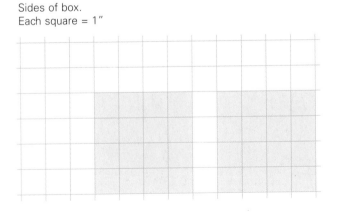

Flower box side pattern

Bottom of box.
Each square = 1"

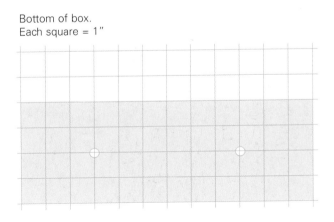

Flower box bottom pattern

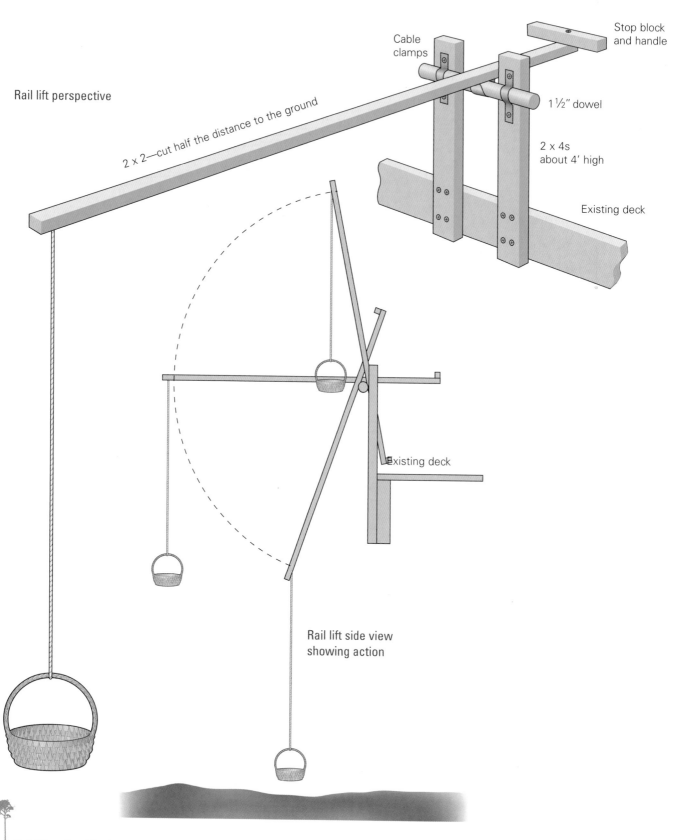

Rail lift perspective

2 x 2—cut half the distance to the ground

Cable clamps

Stop block and handle

1 ½" dowel

2 x 4s about 4' high

Existing deck

Existing deck

Rail lift side view showing action

A solar lamp hanging by the door would be a nice addition. You could buy a metal bracket, but a less expensive way to mount itis to drill a ½-inch hole partway through the door frame near the top and tap in a ½-inch dowel approximately 8 inches long. Also, a solar lamp sunk in the roof will provide after-dark illumination.

Note that candles and kerosene lamps are never used—not even candles on a birthday cake. No fire ever. No exceptions.

Another dowel on the other side gives you a place to hang a bell. And ¼-inch dowels on the inside provide pegs for hanging hats, jackets, and other things.

You must have something to lift small objects and food from the ground. A basket and rope will do at first, but you really should have something nifty with wheels. A couple of options are shown below and at left.

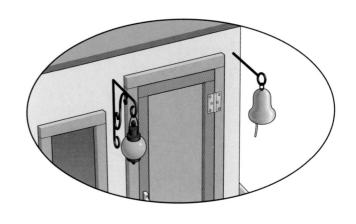

Lamp and bell embellishments

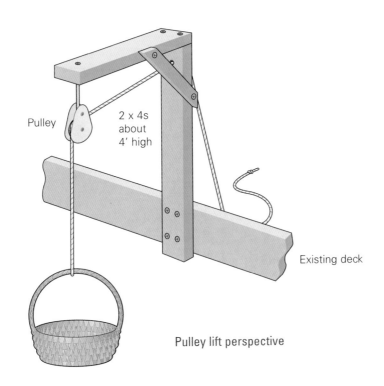

Pulley

2 x 4s about 4' high

Existing deck

Pulley lift perspective

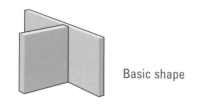

Basic shape

Stool or table

Add three pieces
for a chair.

Small children's furniture may be used, but there are pieces you could put together relatively easily yourself. These are uncomplicated pieces that require no special tools. All are made from pine or plywood and joined with carpenter's glue and screws.

Hang wind chimes on a nearby branch. Leave small objects here and there—such as a box of seashells, beads, or costume jewelry. Don't bother to arrange anything; little fingers will do it all.

Once your treehouse is finished, this is not the end, you know. You have hours and hours ahead of you watching people enjoy your creation. And just as one thing leads to another, one treehouse can lead to another . . . and another and another.

Wall pegs

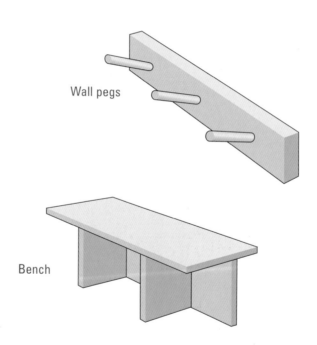

Bench

Chelsea's Gazebo

CHAPTER 10

UNINTENDED CONSEQUENCES

If, like me, you decide to build a little something in a tree and in the process discover that this hobby brings with it loads of enjoyment, it will not be long before other things begin to happen. People will be drawn to your creation. Strangers politely tap on your front door and ask whether they may take a closer look. You may begin to realize that it is an emotional experience for some. The degree of intensity varies widely, but each encounter with visitors is a wonderful shared experience.

EVOLUTION OF A TREEHOUSE VILLAGE

What started as a treehouse for me, over the years, became a treehouse village. Our house sits on a corner lot. The complex begins near the front corner and continues down the side of the house and into the backyard, which contains most of the trees.

The village consists mainly of two groups of structures, all connected by bridges. The only time the entire area is visible from one spot is in the winter when the trees lose their leaves, but the map on page 104 should give you a sense of the relationship of one structure to another.

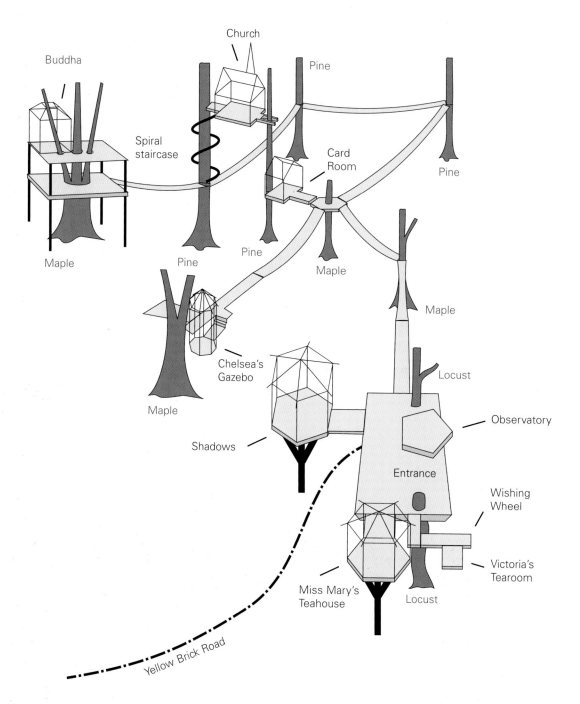

A map of the village

The first group of structures can be seen from the road as you drive by. You have a full view of our flowerbeds, the arbor entrance, the shade gardens, and the freestanding deck out back under the trees.

From the flower-covered arbor, you will find a winding path made with real yellow bricks—the Yellow Brick Road.

The first group of structures is in two locust trees, approximately 6 feet apart, that have been topped, which resulted in a thick, low canopy that engulfs the deck. You may enter by climbing the ladder at the end of the Yellow Brick Road. At the top, you will see the Observatory.

The Observatory

The Observatory is one of my favorite places. This open, five-sided structure was initially built to hold a telescope. Hey, if you are up in a tree, you are that much closer to the moon, planets, and stars. Right? Sadly, I discovered that even during a calm evening with no trace of a breeze, everything

Treehouses from arbor entrance

Brick Road

Shadows

Observatory interior

Wishing Wheel

wiggles constantly. We now use the Observatory for other things, like lunch. Often I go there after dark, when the colored lamps are lit and the mosquitoes don't realize that a victim is up there in the middle of the tree.

Also from the top of the ladder, you can see the Wishing Wheel, the Old Clock, the Juice Box Express, Victoria's Tearoom, Miss Mary's Teahouse, and Shadows.

Miss Mary's Teahouse

Once you climb the ladder, and climb the steps of the stairs, you'll find yourself on a wooden deck high up in the air, where the leaves of the locust trees form a cavern that shuts

Old Clock

Juice Box Express

Miss Mary's Teahouse

Miss Mary's Teahouse interior

Shadows

Shadows interior

out the rest of the world. The little place with the blue door is called Miss Mary's Teahouse. Miss Mary is my one and only granddaughter, so the first house belongs to her. It has a Dutch door, screened windows, a table, six benches, electric lights, and other mysterious objects. To the left are steps leading to Victoria's Tearoom and the Wishing Wheel. On the near right is a crank device that can lift a tray of jasmine tea and sugar cookies from below.

Bridge

Bridge to the Other Place

The half-solid-half-rope bridge that leads to the backyard can be seen clearly from the road, but the next bridge disappears into a wall of leaves. A small visitor named it the "Bridge to the Other Place" a while ago. It was a young lady who came with three friends. She led the group as they ventured forth along the bridge. When she reached the other end of the bridge, she ducked under the leaves, looked ahead, and then turned around to call to her companions, "There's a whole other place over here."

I will never trim those branches, because it is a constant source of delight when a passerby who has never seen our place stops in for a look and then walks out back under the trees and discovers what is there.

The backyard group consists of four places linked by six bridges and a spiral staircase. When arriving there by bridge, you will first step onto a roundish platform that is a junction. To your left is a rope bridge that leads to a large maple tree with a small deck and three steps down to Chelsea's Gazebo

Card Room

Chelsea's Gazebo

Pinecone Express

Card Room seen from the Bridge to the Other Place

(a tiny gazebo for one). Straight ahead is a short wooden walkway that holds the Pinecone Express and at its end a small canopy-covered room with a little table and chairs, called the Card Room.

The Card Room

The Card Room also serves as a room for lunch, a meeting room, a tearoom, or whatever else you wish it to be. Later I built a snack elevator on the walkway. The snack elevator is a simple design consisting of a single rope going over a large overhead wheel and down to a wicker basket filled with some of the many pinecones found in this area. It's known as the Pinecone Express.

To your right is the first of three rope bridges that take you to the bottom of the spiral staircase. At the top, you will find the little church, but if you are not going up, you can simply angle off to your right on the last bridge, which takes you to the first floor of a two-floor open platform.

Spiral staircase looking up to church

The Church in the Pines

This is at the top—my Church in the Pines.

There are things a person remembers from childhood—snapshots in your mind of ordinary events as well as the significant. I have a memory of a long-ago snowfall. It piled in tall soft lumps on the big long-needle pine next door. On a bitter-cold night, those snowy lumps twinkled with bits of reflected light. It was pure magic. And it was there that I imagined my first church in the pines.

Buddha

The last house at the top is called Buddha.

One day while poking around the dollar store, I came across an image of the Buddha. That got me thinking. I have a church; why not a house honoring the Buddha? So I started the process of turning the idea into a physical structure. This new house was to be located on a second-floor corner of a platform. The space was thus restricted to the existing area, which was not that big, but this design works well as a small room. I had a few old dark mahogany panels that were just right for the interior, and I knew I wanted the inside to be dim.

At the bottom, you will find a large rope swing and the very popular zip line.

* * *

And there you have it. I hope this book has been as much of an adventure for you as it has been for me. I wish you all the best with your creation.

Little Church

Buddha

Zip line

Buddha interior

METRIC EQUIVALENTS

(to the nearest mm, 0.1 cm, or 0.01 m)

INCHES	MM	CM	INCHES	MM	CM	INCHES	MM	CM
1/8	3	0.3	9	229	22.9	30	762	76.2
1/4	6	0.6	10	254	25.4	31	787	78.7
3/8	10	1.0	11	279	27.9	32	813	81.3
1/2	13	1.3	12	305	30.5	33	838	83.8
5/8	16	1.6	13	330	33.0	34	864	86.4
3/4	19	1.9	14	356	35.6	35	889	88.9
7/8	22	2.2	15	381	38.1	36	914	91.4
1	25	2.5	16	406	40.6	37	940	94.0
1 1/4	32	3.2	17	432	43.2	38	965	96.5
1 1/2	38	3.8	18	457	45.7	39	991	99.1
1 3/4	44	4.4	19	483	48.3	40	1016	101.6
2	51	5.1	20	508	50.8	41	1041	104.1
2 1/2	64	6.4	21	533	53.3	42	1067	106.7
3	76	7.6	22	559	55.9	43	1092	109.2
3 1/2	89	8.9	23	584	58.4	44	1118	111.8
4	102	10.2	24	610	61.0	45	1143	114.3
4 1/2	114	11.4	25	635	63.5	46	1168	116.8
5	127	12.7	26	660	66.0	47	1194	119.4
6	152	15.2	27	686	68.6	48	1219	121.9
7	178	17.8	28	711	71.1	49	1245	124.5
8	203	20.3	29	737	73.7	50	1270	127.0

CONVERSION FACTORS

1 MM   =   0.039 INCH

1 M   =   3.28 FEET

1 M^2 =   10.8 SQUARE FEET

1 INCH   =   25.4 MM

1 FOOT   =   304.8 MM

1 SQUARE
   FOOT   =   0.09 M^2

MM   =   MILLIMETER

CM   =   CENTIMETER

M   =   METER

M^2 =   SQUARE METER

INDEX

About the Author

Maurice Barkley retired from a career as a commercial artist—and thanks to his children and grandchildren—discovered a new and surprising life as a builder of treehouses. Maurice has had a lifelong fascination with treehouses and the things that go with them, such as rope swings, bridges, secret clubs, and the sound of the wind on a quiet afternoon. Several years ago, it occurred to him that the triple-trunk maple tree in his backyard would support a small platform. This led to what he fondly calls unintended consequences.

As he built the first platform he came to realize that this was enormously fun and gratifying. The act of doing broke down some mental barriers, and ideas began to take shape in his mind. He loved doing it. He could not stop, so he set his sights on the next tree and never looked back, except to admire what he had built. What started as a treehouse, over the years, became a treehouse village.

These days, unintended but wonderful consequences abound for Maurice and his wife, Marie. Their circle of friends is now as wide as the globe we all live on.

The path Marie and Maurice now travel stretches well beyond the horizon, and both are eager to see what lies beyond the next bend.

The treehouse village has been featured on the HGTV program *Look What I Did!* and is a destination in the international adventure of Geocaching.

Maurice's Web site is: www.mystrees.com